About the author

Before his untimely death Kees Epskamp (1950–2003) was a major contributor to
the evolution of Theatre for Development as a key element in Culture and Development studies. His theoretical understanding of this field was rooted in practical
educational projects in South America and Africa.

His academic journey began as a student of Social Anthropology at Leiden
University, progressed through a PhD in Political and Cultural Sciences from the
University of Amsterdam for a dissertation (1989) published as *Theatre in Search of
Social Change*, and led him to posts as consultant to the Utrecht School of the Arts
(1994–2002) and external examiner of the MA course in Theatre for Development
at King Alfred's University College (2000–2002).

His practical work involved technical assistance to Culture and Development
projects involving Theatre for Development in Zimbabwe, the Netherlands and
Costa Rica. The last position he held was with the National UNESCO Commission
of the Netherlands, as coordinator of World Heritage (2001–3).

In the final days of his life, aware that the curtain would fall before the play
was over, Kees asked a longstanding friend and colleague, Ad Boeren, to play a
role in finishing the manuscript. With the help of Marjanne Paardekooper, Rien
Sprenger and Emile Schra, Ad has been able to finish Kees's book, and hopes that
the result will serve the purpose which the author had in mind.

Theatre *for* Development

An introduction to Context,
Applications and Training

KEES EPSKAMP

With a Foreword by Tim Prentki

Netherlands organization for international
cooperation in higher education

Zed Books
LONDON AND NEW YORK

Zed Books and the author gratefully acknowledge the generous support of the following organisations which enabled the publication of this book.

Netherlands Organization for International Cooperation in Higher Education (NUFFIC), based in The Hague, The Netherlands
Netherlands National Commission for UNESCO, based in The Hague, The Netherlands
Theatre Embassy, based in Amsterdam, The Netherlands

Foreword copyright © Tim Prentki 2006
© Kees Epskamp 2006

Theatre for development was first published by Zed Books Ltd,
7 Cynthia Street, London N1 9JF, UK and Room 400, 175 Fifth Avenue,
New York, NY 10010, USA in 2006
www.zedbooks.co.uk

© Kees Epskamp 2006

Cover designed by Andrew Corbett
Set in 10/13 pt Photina by Long House, Cumbria, UK
Printed and bound in Malta by Gutenberg Press Ltd

Distributed in the USA exclusively by Palgrave Macmillan, a division of
St Martin's Press, LLC, 175 Fifth Avenue, New York, NY 10010

The right of Kees Epskamp to be identified as the author of this work has been asserted by him in accordance with the Copyright, Designs and Patents Act, 1988

A catalogue record for this book is available from the British Library

US Cataloging-in-Publication Data is available from the Library of Congress

ISBN 1 84277 732 7 (hb)   ISBN 978 1 84277 732 9 (hb)
ISBN 1 84277 733 5 (pb)   ISBN 978 1 84277 733 6 (pb)

Contents

Part I
Theatre for Development: History, Practice and Prospects

Part II
Essays on Development, Education and the Arts

Boxes, Tables & Figures

Boxes

Tables

Figures

Acronyms
& Abbreviations

ACAE	African Council of Adult Education
ACFOD	Asian Cultural Forum on Development
ACPC	Action for Cultural and Political Change (India)
ACPTA	African Centre for the Training of Performing Arts
AFSYMWORK	Africa Symposium Workshop
ALAE	African Council of Adult Education
AMI	Academy of Indonesian Music
AREPP	African Research and Educational Puppetry Programme
ARTPAD	A Resource for Theatre and Participatory Development
ASKI	Akademi Seni Karawitan Indonesia
ASTI	Akademi Seni Tar Indonesia (National Academy of Indonesian Dance)
ATB	Atelier-Théâtre Burkinabè
ATEX	African Theatre Exchange
AusAID	The Australian Government's Overseas Aid Program
BaMa	Bachelor-Master (structure)
BC	British Council
CBO	Community Based Organisation
CDC	Centre for Development Communications (King Alfred's Winchester University College, UK)
cdcArts	Centre for the Arts in Development Communications (School of Community and Performing Arts, King Alfred's College, Winchester, UK)
CEASPA	Centre of Studies and Social Action (Costa Rica)
CEE	Centre for Environmental Education (India)
CESO	Centre for the Study of Education in Developing Countries (Netherlands)
CIDA	Canadian International Development Agency
CONFINTEA V	Fifth World Conference on Adult Education
CPR	Centre for Peformance Research (University of Wales, UK)
CVPA	Centre of Visual and Performing Arts (Namibia)

DAC	Development Assistance Committee
DANIDA	Danish International Development Agency
DfID	Department for International Development (United Kingdom)
DGIS	Dutch Directorate General of International Cooperation
DSC	Development Support Communication
DSE	Deutsche Stiftung für Entwicklung (German Foundation for International Development)
ESA	European Sociological Association
EU	European Union
FAO	Food and Agriculture Organization of the United Nations
FITD	International Theatre Festival for Development
GO	Governmental Organisation
GTZ	Deutsche Gesellschaft für Technische Zusammenarbeit (German Foundation for International Development)
HEI	Higher Educational Institute
HIVOS	Humanistisch Instituut voor Ontwikkelingssamenwerking (Netherlands)
HKU	Utrecht School of the Arts
HRD	Human Resource Development
IATA	International Amateur Theatre Association
ICAE	International Council of Adult Education
IDEA	International Drama / Theatre and Education Association
IKJ	Institut Kesenian Jakarta (Indonesia)
IMF	International Monetary Fund
IPTA	International Popular Theatre Alliance
IPTA	Indian People's Theatre Association
IPTA	Indigenous People's Theater Association
ISI	Institute of Indonesian Arts
ITB	Technology Institute of Bandung (Indonesia)
ITI	International Theatre Institute (Paris, France)
JICA	Japan International Cooperation Agency
KAC	King Alfred's University College (Winchester, UK)
KDEA	Kenya Drama / Theatre and Education Association
KIT	Royal Tropical Institute (Netherlands)
LBDA	Lake Basin Development Authority (Kenya)
LGM	Learner-Generated Materials
MA	Master of Arts
MADC	Museo de Arte y Deseño Contemporáneo (Costa Rica)
MDBs	Multilateral Development Banks
MECATE	Movimiento de Expresíon Campesino Artística (Mexico)
MOEC	Ministry of Education and Culture
MONDIACULT	World Conference on Cultural Policies
NFED	Non-Formal Education Division
NGO	Non-Governmental Organisation
NNGOs	Northern NGOs
NORAD	Norwegian Agency for Development Cooperation
NPOs	Non-Profit Organisations

OECD	Organization for Economic Cooperation and Development
PAT	Programme Advisory Team
PCM	Project Cycle Management
PET	People's Educational Theatre (Swaziland)
PETA	Philippine Educational Theatre Association
PLA	Participatory Learning Activities
POs	People's Organisations
PPP	Participatory Performance Practices
PRA	Participatory Rural Appraisal
PVOs	Private Voluntary Organisations
QUANGOs	Quasi Non-Governmental Organisations
R&D	Research & Development
RDWSSP	Rural Domestic Water Supply and Sanitation Programme (Kenya)
RRA	Rapid Rural Appraisal
SAGs	Social Action Groups
SAPs	Structural Adjustment Programmes
SEAMEO	South-East Asian Ministers of Education Organisation
SIDA	Swedish International Development Cooperation Agency
SNGOs	Southern NGOs
SPAFA	SEAMEO Regional Centre for Archaeology and Fine Arts
STDs	Sexually Transmitted Diseases
STSI	National College of Indonesian Arts
SWAp	Sector-Wide Approach
SWOT	Strengths, Weaknesses, Opportunities and Threats
TEC	Teatro Experimental de Cali (Colombia)
TfD	Theatre for Development
TIE	Theatre-in-Education
TREE	Theatre for Research Education and Empowerment (Bangladesh)
UAPA	Union of African Performing Artists
UL	Leiden University
UN	United Nations
UNDP	United Nations Development Programme
UNESCO	United Nations Educational, Scientific and Culture Organisation
UNFPA	United nations Fund for Population Activities
UNHCR	United Nations High Commissioner for Refugees
UNICEF	United nations Children's Fund
UNZA	University of Zambia
UvA	University of Amsterdam
WB	World Bank
WCCD	World Commission on Culture and Development
WDCD	United Nations World Decade for Cultural Development
WHO	World Heath Organization
ZACT	Zimbabwe Association for Community Theatres
ZANTAA	Zambian National Theatre Arts Association
ZBC	Zambia Broadcasting Corporation
ZOPP	Zielorientierte Projekt Planung

Acknowledgements

This publication states the author's personal standpoint on various polemics in the field of development studies and the arts. Several case studies (presented in the boxes) are based on personal field and documentary explorations. A number of chapters are the result of inspiring dialogues held with colleagues from the Utrecht School of the Arts (HKU) and the School of Community and Performing Arts at King Alfred's University College (KAC), Winchester.

The author would like to acknowledge the University of Utrecht, especially the Anthropology Department, for the fruitful academic exchange that colleagues and students provided during workshop meetings of the inter-university diploma course 'Education in Developing Countries'.

This book would have never been completed without the encouragement of the author's wife, Marjanne Paardekooper. The author is grateful to Ross Kidd for stimulating and sharpening memories going back more than twenty years, and to Jet Vos for information provided on Forum Theatre in Kenya. The sections in this book referring to 'stakeholder analysis' have been inspired by informal communication with Loukie Levert. Ron Kukler is thanked for checking and updating the information presented in the case study materials on Namibia, and Rieks Smeets for his support in bringing the study to the point of publication. The author also thanks Eugène van Erven, Alex Mavrocordatos, Matthew Cohen and Han Vermeulen for their brief but fruitful comments.

Parts and sections of this book have been reprinted from earlier articles in magazines and journals. Parts have been reprinted from 'The Role of Education in Cultural and Artistic Development', published as Chapter 8 of the *International Yearbook of Education*, 1994 (pp. 158–72); 'Art Education and Cultural Identity', published in 1996 in Leo Dubbeldam and Kees Epskamp (eds) *Searching Together: an Anthology of Educational Research in China and the Netherlands* (CESO paperback no. 20), pp. 225–44; 'Caro o Mascara', a paper presented at the Conference on 'The Voice of the Artists at the End of the Millennium: Our Proposals for a Cultural Agenda', San José, Costa Rica, 22–24 July 1996; 'Cultural Identity: Mask or True

Face?', a paper presented at the Third European Conference of the European Socio-logical Association (ESA), 27–30 August 1997, University of Essex, Colchester, UK; 'Healing Divided Societies', published in 1999 in *People Building Peace: 35 Inspiring Stories from Around the World*, a publication of the European Centre for Conflict Prevention in cooperation with the International Fellowship of Reconciliation (Utrecht: European Centre for Conflict Prevention); 'Community Theatre: Local and National Identity Building', in 2000 in John O'Toole and Margret Lepp (eds) *Drama for Life: Stories of Adult Learning and Empowerment* (Brisbane: Playlab Press), pp. 125–34.

Special mention must be made of the financial support provided by the Nether-lands Organization for International Cooperation in Higher Education (NUFFIC), Netherlands National (The Hague) and the Theatre Embassy (Amsterdam) Commission for UNESCO, without which the publication of this book would have been impossible.

Ad Boeren

Marjanne Paardekooper would like to acknowledge the careful and creative work of Ad Boeren, who completed her husband's manuscript and brought this book to the verge of publication.

To Joep and Emma

Foreword

Theatre for Development (TfD) – whereby communities are enabled to address issues of self-development through participation in a theatre process – has grown in ubiquity, accessibility and importance over four decades. It began in the 1970s as a strategy for popular education with adults and children in sub-Saharan Africa, the Indian subcontinent and Latin America. Today the contexts for its application have spread throughout the world, either in its own name or under the currently fashionable term of 'applied theatre', wherever there is scope for informal and non-formal education to attempt to improve the lives of the disadvantaged. Non-governmental organisations (NGOs) are playing an increasing role in civil societies across the globe and – since their initial, somewhat mechanistic, post-war interventions in areas such as agriculture, infrastructure and health – have come to acknowledge the key roles that communication and creativity play in any effective strategy for self-development. This realisation has brought with it a developing profile for TfD as a methodology that is participatory, not resource-intensive, and not dependent upon the literacy of its participants or audiences. Many of the major international NGOs now use TfD routinely as part of their policies for addressing issues such as behaviour change in relation to AIDS prevention or for conflict resolution.

In spite of these developments there continues to be a tendency for development agencies to view TfD practitioners with suspicion; and for practitioners to earn this suspicion through their ignorance of the aims and methods of those agencies. 'Theatre' and 'development' have circled each other like wary boxers in search of an opening to score points at the expense of the other. NGO personnel frequently regard the artists and academics who work in TfD as out of touch with the realities with which they have to grapple on a daily basis, while they are themselves viewed as inflexible, uncreative and incapable of responding to the aspirations of their target beneficiaries. It is in this area of mutual misunderstanding that Kees Epskamp's work has served a vital function. Throughout his career he straddled both these worlds and worked tirelessly as both a practitioner and a theoretician to demonstrate the dialectical relationships between the two.

The cornerstone of his vision is the potential of arts education to unlock the creative capacity of the individual and so change social relations within the community. For Kees both development and theatre are aspects of the same process: one whereby individuals and communities are able to transform themselves from the objects into the subjects of their own development. He devoted his professional life to the practice, study and recording of this process with all the modesty, care and reflection that typified the man.

In the Introduction to *Theatre in Search of Social Change*, published in 1989, Kees wrote:

> In this book I intend to contribute both to the theory and the practice of theatre for development. In the first place by presenting a historical reconstruction of its conceptualisation. In the second place, in the case studies I hope to place theatre for development, as an integration of two autonomous phenomena – theatre and development – in the context of history and local culture, in such a way that the continuous process of social change of the last four decades in the North Atlantic world as well as in the Third World are properly taken into account, to enable the researcher, theatre maker or development worker to assess its impact and educative value. (Epskamp, 1989: 14)

In his own person he combined the roles of researcher, theatre maker and development worker, and this publication – together with his years of work at the Centre for the Study of Education in Developing Countries (CESO) – made an immense contribution towards the refocusing of popular theatre as the genre now known as Theatre for Development. Whilst it is now becoming more common for practitioners to have experience of both popular or applied theatre and of development, Kees was one of those rare pioneers, along with Michael Etherton, who engaged professionally in both worlds and was therefore able to offer an informed critique of the practices of each. In consequence agencies engaged in the processes of development have come increasingly to appreciate the importance of communication and creativity in achieving sustainable human development goals, while those practising theatre oriented to social change have understood the importance of connecting community theatre work to other grassroots initiatives and to global economic realities if any discernible, lasting impact is to follow from these activities.

The present volume is both a companion and a sequel to the earlier book and further enhances Kees's international reputation as the foremost researcher and documenter of TfD of his generation. It was my all-too-brief privilege to work alongside him when he was appointed external examiner of the MA in Theatre for Development at King Alfred's College (now the MA in Theatre and Media for Development at the University of Winchester). The wealth of his knowledge was inexhaustible and he was always able to provide a cross-reference, case study or supporting example when discussion turned to what had been done at other times and in other places. Yet this knowledge and understanding was delivered with humility and modesty to the point of self-effacement. His interventions were marked by a desire to do the best for the students and to improve the design and delivery of the curriculum. The role of education in developing potential, building capacity and releasing creativity was close to his heart. The layout of this monograph reflects the man. First comes the meticulous and comprehensive research and documentation. Only after the reader has had an opportunity to digest this cornucopia of information (Chapters 1 to 6) does he venture to offer his own understandings and interpretations (the essays that make up Chapters 7 to 12) expressed in a typically understated and careful manner.

As Kees observes both in this volume and elsewhere, TfD is a process of social analysis and as such can never be complete. There is no such thing as a definitive statement of purpose or of practice. Instead he offers us a cogent summary of the achievements of the genre in the last quarter of the twentieth century and a secure platform from which to take stock of what has and has not been done. The essays offer some pointers to the challenges facing facilitators of cultural interventions in the new millennium but inevitably big issues have emerged in the period since the completion of the manuscript that TfD is just beginning to address.

Contradictions – between power and dignity, and between justice and freedom – have always been at the heart of TfD practice. Once individuals and communities begin to tell stories grounded in their real-life experiences, these contradictions, fuelled by the emotional possibilities of performance, form the barriers to self-actualisation. Such a contradiction lies, for example, at the heart of the famous play *Ngaahika Ndeenda* ('I Will Marry When I Want') produced by Ngugi wa Thiong'o and Ngugi wa Mirii for the Kamiriithu Community Educational and Cultural Centre in 1977 (Ngugi wa Thiong'o and Ngugi wa Mirii, 1982). Today this contradiction is increasingly expressed through the ever more overt discrepancies opening up between the neoliberal economic agenda by which all the governments of the world are more or less enthralled, and the framework of universal human rights to which these same governments subscribe but on which they cannot deliver within the dominant economic structures.

TfD as a practical form of social analysis has to find ways to connect its micro-practices at the local level with the macro-agendas that directly impact upon the lives of the participants in those practices. For example, a needs-based approach to poverty reduction – the primary target of many development initiatives – is likely to leave the underlying neocolonial dependency paradigm unchanged, whereas a rights-based approach might, via a practical analysis of structural adjustment, raise a plethora of interrelated questions around governance, democracy, justice and equity: questions that require a new paradigm. Globalisation presents development agencies and hence TfD with new challenges on an almost daily basis. Former, at least partially stable notions of community have had to be revised in the wake of global and internal migration that locates the global in the local and the local in the global. What were once impassable distinctions between First and Third Worlds and between the South and the North are now porous, resulting in angry juxtapositions of wealth and poverty in all parts of the globe. TfD has to respond to these new geographies by recognising potential applications as they emerge next door as well as on the other side of the world.

As a core method for the participation and mobilisation of all sectors of communities, TfD will have to address the growing crisis of the alienation of young people which manifests itself in different forms in different societies: the child soldiers and child witches of Africa; the sex workers of East Asia; young people in Europe and North America who have lost the capacity for social play and imagination through an isolated, virtual existence interacting with images on screens. Agencies and theatre groups who continue to behave as if this was not the present reality will quickly discover that their interventions are redundant. Over and above all these considerations hangs the environmental threat to the planet posed by our inability to change the way we live in response to the realities of climate change, overpopulation and the terminal exhaustion of finite resources by land and sea. If the great strength and potential of TfD is its capacity to initiate a process of behaviour change, this is the arena in which its greatest test will surely lie.

The years ahead will call for a fundamental reconsideration of what it is to be human: how we live; why we live. The economic models to which we have grown used – be these communist or capitalist – will no longer offer the prospect of prosperity or even survival. Kees Epskamp's life and work serves as a timely reminder of those capacities upon which we shall need to draw as we engage in these processes of redefinition: imagination, creativity, communication and, above all, humility. Many of us found in Kees the unflagging inspiration to continue the work of trying to create a fairer, more secure world for the majority of its people.

Tim Prentki
Professor of Theatre for Development
University of Winchester

Introduction

> Once upon a time, not so very long ago, when the West was a good deal more sure of itself, of what it was, and what it wasn't, the concept of culture had a firm design and a definite edge. (Geertz, 1996: 42)

When launching the results of my study *Theatre in Search of Social Change* (December 1989), I was hardly aware of the implications of the fall of the Berlin Wall one month earlier and the way my book fitted into a historic epoch which had just come to a conclusion.[1] This event implied the end of the Cold War, which since the 1950s had divided not only the First and Second Worlds but also determined the boundaries of the Third World by enforcing political and cultural choices between capitalist consumerism and communist state monopolism. Moreover, a period of very undemocratic decision making by dictatorial regimes in numerous developing countries, as well as economic and cultural domination by imperialist forces, had ceased. A new era was heralded in which centralist state planning would be dismantled while state enterprises and public services were privatised in line with the liberalisation of market mechanisms. This had its implications for 'culture and development' policies, though the results would only be noticeable at the beginning of the twenty-first century.

During the 1960s and 1970s there was in many South-East Asian, African and Central American nations strong left-wing opposition to mainstream governments. In Central America popular movements opposed right-wing dictators and juntas (regimes consisting of high-ranking military officers) as political liberation movements and student or labour organisations resisted violent oppression. These movements were at the heart of political processes aimed at democratisation.

During the 1970s cultural activities including theatre did indeed contribute to the fall of the Marcos regime in the Philippines and the Samosa regime in Nicaragua. Artists and theatre activists such as Augusto Boal (Brazil, Argentina, Peru) and the novelist-playwright Ngugi wa Thiong'o[2] (Kenya) had to go into exile, though some later returned to their homeland.

In the North Atlantic world the avant-garde vanished during the 1980s with the turn to postmodernism. However, in the Third World there were and still are artists and intellectuals with a strong commitment towards changing society and ending social inequality. Among them are performing artists, dancers, directors, actors, musicians, composers, puppeteers and storytellers with a vanguard role within the political and cultural development of their countries. Several theatre directors and groups have made an enormous impact by breaking with Western-

oriented theatre concepts to assert and develop local forms of expression. A growing number of artists have explored the harsh realities of modern life in the fight for democracy and social equality.

Postmodern debate

Political change during the 1960s and 1970s had consequences for the role of science and arts in society. Many scholars noticed that academic research did not always offer solutions to urgent and immediate problems and turned to action research, a methodological school that seeks solutions to concrete problems and conflicts where conventional social scientific research focuses on solutions to hypothetical problems. Since then action research has been used to assist in identifying the relationships between the subjective and objective at the heart of the post-positivist debate in the social sciences, also referred to as the postmodern debate.

Whereas modern scientific understanding and faith in linear progress towards a better world was marked by a strong belief in the Enlightenment concept (Man as the measure of all things), postmodern social sciences lost faith in the grand narratives underlying dominant world ideologies such as Marxism, capitalism and humanism. The strong socialist belief in a 'man-made society' that had been prominent in European politics from the 1960s proved an illusion.

Postmodern cultural relativism as developed during the 1980s emphasised that there are various layers of reality, expressed by any number of perspectives. As a consequence, it had to be accepted that all cultures contributed equally valid interpretations of reality; and that each culture can only be properly understood and interpreted in its own terms. No longer could all cultures, viewed as different ways of seeing the world, be understood in the same terms.

Within the arts postmodernism contributed to the vanishing of sharp boundaries between formalistic and popular art. According to Copeland (1983: 37), postmodernism led to a more flexible attitude towards popular culture, and a greater accessibility.

These major changes of approach had considerable consequences for the development of the social sciences and the arts at the turn of the twenty-first century.

Theatre for Development

Theatre for Development (henceforth TfD) has been experimented with worldwide in the context of development cooperation, ever since most of the present African nations became independent. TfD, therefore, has a history of little more than four decades. It initially evolved from activities within the field of (non-formal) education and development support communication. This fact in itself has influenced its history.

From the 1970s on local media (especially the performing arts) have been experimented with as tools for development support communication. These initiatives fitted in with community-development strategies focused on'self-reliance' and 'small-scale' development projects. The rationale was that the local media were already available, inexpensive to work with, and well known to the community. The fit with the local culture enabled development workers to illustrate techniques in a way that made them clear and accessible. In this manner TfD came into being either as a direction and persuasion by means of theatre performances or as participatory learning through TfD workshops. Either way, the focus was on changing the behaviour of people.

During the 1960s and 1970s TfD was seen as a form of popular theatre serving awareness-raising processes, and of information practices in suburban as well as in rural communities. Nowadays, it has reached an independent status as a learning strategy in which theatre is used to encourage communities to express their own concerns and reflect upon the causes of their problems and possible solutions. All these types of theatre, however, deal with (national) developmental issues in relation to local problems and situations.

The present publication is meant to be a general introduction for tertiary-level students and staff in the fields of development studies, performing arts studies and education (especially in developing countries). It also hopes to attract policy planners, programme managers and development practitioners (governmental as well as non-governmental), drama teachers, TfD facilitators and adult educators. The main goals of the study are: (1) to contextualise TfD historically within a wider range of development theories, strategies and practices; and (2) to synthesise practical and innovative experiences gained with different approaches in TfD projects and programmes. The research underlying my arguments has not been undertaken from the perspective of theatre studies or literary criticism, but from that of development studies: a cross-disciplinary knowledge domain drawing from other disciplines including arts and literature studies (such as history, drama and performance studies) and social and political sciences (including anthropology and sociology).

Structure and contents

The present study is divided into two. Part I consists of six chapters sketching and discussing the role and place of TfD in development processes unfolding over the last four decades. The story is told from the perspective of development cooperation and cultural development. Part II consists of six essays on topics touching upon the wider context in which TfD has developed and is being applied. These essays try to create a better understanding both of the forces that have influenced the development of TfD and of its theoretical insertion within cultural and development studies. The essays in Part II can be read separately or in conjunction with the chapters of Part I.

Part I: TfD

Chapter 1 presents the reader with a concise early history of TfD, the international networking and collaboration, and the way this form of drama has been applied during four decades. It introduces some of the crucial initiatives undertaken in Africa during the 1970s. Here decisive experiments were launched by a small group of foreign employees ('expatriates') attached to university English or Drama departments, sometimes referred to as 'Performing Arts' departments. Staff members of these universities were familiar with and inevitably influenced each other's work.

Chapter 2 discusses TfD in two different contexts: development approaches and cultural policies. In the first context, a distinction is made between conventional and participatory approaches to development that will shape the book's evolving discourse when addressing such topics as whether TfD should be used as a product or a process. Historically, the distinction between conventional and participatory approaches to development goes back to the critique that emerged during the 1970s of state-directed, centralised development. This criticism resulted in the move towards more people-oriented initiatives for change. NGOs especially have experimented with small-scale and participatory projects in which the local community and the primary stakeholders were stimulated to become actors in their own development process instead of objects of someone else's development agenda. In the past, development was perceived as the endeavour of the national governments of individual developing countries. More recently, however, development has been perceived as the collective responsibility of all stakeholding parties involved: government, private sector and civil society. A search for new support modalities has begun.

The other context in which TfD is discussed has to do with cultural policies and the way these have developed over the years. During the 1950s, culture was seen as a factor of resistance, a formidable opponent to change. The 'traditional way of life' was an obstacle to be overcome by all possible means, in order to harvest the fruits of modernity: wealth, health and respect in an ever-widening circle of developed nations.

This view of culture as an obstacle to social change and development has slowly evolved into its opposite. It is generally accepted that nowadays culture presents a facilitating environment to development. As the way of life of a community is largely determined by cultural factors, it is not possible to intervene in its development without taking cultural beliefs and practices into account.

This second chapter presents a state-of-the-practice review of the role of culture in development and the implications of current thinking for international donor support towards the (performing) arts and cultural development as a small-scale training device in the field of development support communication.

Chapter 3 deals with two major applications of TfD: as a learning process and as a product used for learning. The generic term TfD describes a range of theatrical practices and participatory methods to engage marginalised members of communities in a dialogical process. Thereby one aims to enhance awareness of political and social issues, build up social cohesion and stimulate the participation, awareness, and organisational strength of groups, communities and organisations. However, these practices and methods can be applied in different ways.

Using TfD as a learning and discovery process, as a sequence of social practices seen as interconnected, the aim is to create critical consciousness and to raise the participants' awareness of the possibility of taking action to solve their development problems. In this sense, TfD is always 'work in progress'.

On the other hand, change can be achieved by using TfD performances to provide communities with information in order to influence their way of thinking on certain topics and may lead to behavioural changes. Both applications enjoy considerable success, either separately or combined.

Chapter 4 looks at the conditions to be created and recognised in order to bring about a successful application of TfD as a learning process and a product for learning. This success depends on many factors. There needs to be room for genuine participation, sound basic conditions for local ownership, cultural openness to the approach as well as practical opportunities to use TfD. These critical conditions are discussed in a systematic way, using a logical framework analysis. Attention is also paid to the intricate relationship between empowerment and participatory processes and to the important role which facilitators and socio-cultural constraints play in TfD.

In Chapter 5 the rather limited opportunities for education and training in TfD are discussed. To make TfD sustainable as a development support communication device there is a constant need for training programmes to provide for capacity building in this field and to train trainers, facilitators, animators or coaches. Whether in the North or in the South, there are few examples of higher educational training institutes showing special commitment in their curricula to 'Research and Development' (R&D) into the use of performing arts in development support communication. The best examples to date are to be found in the North.

Several universities in developing countries include a national school of drama or courses in drama and performance studies. Some also provide degrees in the field of cultural management, organisation and administration. To present a more extensive insight into the curricula of these programmes, the contents of a number of specific courses offered in India and sub-Saharan Africa are discussed. The chapter also presents a selection of higher educational training institutes in the South as well as in the North that show a special commitment to training and research into the use of (performing) arts in development support communication.

Chapter 6, concluding Part I, brings together the theories, strategies and practices presented in the foregoing chapters. Taking stock of the role which TfD has played in processes of socio-economic and cultural development over the years, it discusses the strengths and weaknesses of TfD as an instrument in social change processes and the influence of local contexts on its utilisation. It touches on the shift from a recipe towards a partnership approach in development cooperation, in which the concept of ownership plays an important part. In addition, this chapter looks forward, sighting opportunities and pitfalls for the use of TfD in development projects and programmes before stating a brief agenda for further action.

Part II: essays on development, education and the arts

The first essay in Part II (Chapter 7) deals in more detail with various development approaches used by donors and NGOs and their underlying ideologies. The essay also discusses the planning and management processes characteristic of more conventional development projects and programmes.

The second essay (Chapter 8) pays attention to various dimensions involved when assessing the results of development activities. Monitoring and evaluation studies are integrated into projects and programmes in order to inform the project staff and/or the sponsor about the effectiveness of various project activities. The importance of indicators and baseline surveys and benchmarks is also discussed.

TfD is all about awareness raising, learning, communication and action. As such it occupies a specific niche in broader communication and educational strategies. TfD is only one of many communication media used for development purposes. In the third essay (Chapter 9), TfD is juxtaposed with a wider range of media used in processes of social intervention in developing countries. In order to enthuse 'primary stakeholders', projects and programmes apply various communication strategies, including mobilisation campaigns, awareness raising (using dramatisation by a theatre group), etcetera.

The fourth essay (Chapter 10) looks at educational systems in general. It explains the differences between formal, non-formal and informal types of education, paying special attention to adult education, to which Theatre for Development is most strongly related.

The final two essays draw the reader's attention to the importance of the arts for society, the cultural identity of ethnic groups and mediation processes between cultures and groups in conflict. The fifth essay (Chapter 11) relates the curriculum of art education within regular school programmes to the national artistic environment. In giving time and space to arts and cultural activities schools not only introduce knowledge of culture through cultural experience, but also impart aesthetic knowing as a form of knowledge in itself, on a par with scientific knowledge. This can only be achieved if the arts and culture are taken seriously within a generally progressive formal as well as non-formal educational framework. Through their arts experience, children and young adults learn about themselves and others.

The final essay (Chapter 12) discusses the manner in which visual and performing arts have been used to address violent conflicts and civil wars all over the world. Attention is paid to the role of the arts in conflict prevention and in processes of change and social development related to conflict management. Apart from applying the arts to support the creation of a just society, many development practitioners use techniques derived from artistic creation for problem-solving purposes at community level.

Part I

Theatre for Development:
History, Practice and Prospects

1

A Contemporary History
of TfD

'The capacity to project imaginatively into a situation and to identify with another perspective enables people to explore human experience in drama . . .' (Donelan, 1999: 256)

To write an introductory chapter on the early history of TfD is a delicate matter: many talented and critical contemporaries participated in some, if not all, of the main events described. It is not my intention to present a detailed history of TfD. The way the early history is presented here is based on a personal perspective woven into a more general discourse, taking my field experiences and active participation in workshops, seminars and conferences as points of departure. In tribute to fellow researchers, an attempt has been made to relate my findings to their writings by means of notes to be found at the conclusion of this book (pp. 154–9). Two pioneers should be foregrounded in this context, because of their efforts to develop and systematise some of the didactic principles used during the 1960s and 1970s: Paolo Freire, the Brazilian adult educator and philosopher, and theatre director Augusto Boal.

During the 1960s Freire experimented in Brazil with innovative and participatory learning methods within the context of adult education and literacy training. During the next decade these ideas inspired his fellow-countryman Boal to experiment with applied forms of drama, stimulating the active participation of audience members and supporting them in awareness training and problem solving at community level. Boal's writings have contributed powerfully to the further development of TfD to date. Nowadays TfD is considered a developmental intervention tool to be used within the context of non-formal education and/or development support communication to support processes of social change.

Defining TfD

TfD is a relatively recent phenomenon. Its pre-history began in Western Europe during the 1960s as 'popular theatre', 'people's theatre' or even 'activist theatre'. All these terms remind us of the period before the end of the Cold War (1989), and

Box 1.1 Paolo Freire

Professional literature, policy documents and case studies on non-formal education, literacy and adult education can often be traced back to Paolo Freire's *Pedagogy of the Oppressed* (1972), emphasising the view that education requires communication in the form of starting a continuing dialogue between the learners or trainees and their trainers, teachers, animators or facilitators.[3]

Freire started in the late 1960s and early 1970s to develop a pedagogy of liberation with peasants in Brazil. Since then, his methodology and techniques of political mobilisation have also served other purposes – for example, in awareness raising on issues concerning the environment, health and family planning. Freire was concerned not with individual autonomy, but with empowering groups of people to take charge of their political and social environment.

In his view literacy training was the only way out for the poor, providing a voice to the voiceless and breaking away from the 'culture of silence'. Learning to read and write would provide the learners with an opportunity to relate the use of abstract signs (the written word) to their own everyday existence. Participants in literacy classes not only learn to read and write, but are also made conscious of the repressive structure of society and their own (oppressed) position. Through this critical reflection upon society, they should arrive at collective action in order to change things in society.

Freire holds the opinion that educative programmes – including literacy and numeracy – should contain a political component, implicitly or explicitly. According to his pedagogics, education cannot be neutral: it is focused either on the consolidation of the existing (oppressive) regime, or on the liberation or emancipation of the people.

The people should become aware of these two conflicting tendencies. The only way in which they could do so – according to Freire – was by becoming literate. Freire himself used the concept of 'conscientisation' instead of awareness training. This concept, introduced by Freire during the early 1980s, is now widely used to refer to the process of raising people's self-awareness through collective self-inquiry and reflection, and transforming that reality by collective action.[4] Ultimately this should provide people with the skills to participate actively in a democratic society.

In Freire's idea, the oppressed illiterates must be offered the opportunity to become conscious of the fact they can change their own situation. To do so they have to take their own life experiences as points of departure for their education. First, everybody must experience 'standing up and speaking out loud'. Second, participants have to learn to listen, analyse and react to others. In short, they must learn what it means to enter upon a 'dialogue' with others.

refer to the application of performing arts as a 'weapon' used strongly and explicitly to oppose political and social oppression. The practitioners of these forerunner genres of TfD had a very pronounced socialist or Marxist perspective. Therefore, in defining these terms political or ideological references are almost always involved.

Other terms nowadays used for TfD projects are Theatre in Education (TIE) projects or Community Theatre projects. All these fields overlap. Which of the three applies best to a particular project depends on definitions of the terms 'development', 'education' or 'community' . TfD is mostly used in the context of 'development support communication' and/or in the field of adult education and training. Theatre in Education (TIE) basically refers to the use of theatre within a formal school or out-of-school context. According to Jackson (1997: 49–50) TIE began in Britain during the mid-1960s and spread rapidly as theatres sought to extend their outreach programmes and developed a variety of ways of speaking to the communities they served. TIE refers to the use of theatre for explicit educational purposes, closely allied to the school curriculum and mostly in educational contexts: schools, colleges and youth clubs, or sometimes museums and historic sites.

Community theatre refers to theatre initiatives taken and further developed by the community itself, most often based on local forms of indigenous theatre or performing arts within the community.

All three types of theatre are participatory in nature.

In response to these different concepts the Royal Tropical Institute (KIT) in Amsterdam introduced a conceptual common denominator: 'theatre and development'.[5] Under this conceptual umbrella various applied forms of drama are brought together, including TfD. This definitely has its advantages. It offers a way of avoiding terminological problems and of focusing on the practicalities of the approach. On the other hand, use of a descriptive denominator such as 'theatre and development' impoverishes the historical depth of the evolution of TfD and widens the field to any form of drama or theatre used within the context of development, even new literary works or mainstream theatre plays.

Perhaps less objectionable would be the use of the term 'participatory theatre' as a common denominator for all sorts of participatory forms of performing arts and applied drama, including TfD, Theatre in Education, Community Theatre and Forum Theatre. All these forms have certain common features: (1) performances or workshops aim at an exchange of ideas between actors/facilitators and the audience; (2) the content of the performances is directly related to the living environment of the targeted audience; (3) the themes interwoven in the storylines of the performances are problem-oriented and of direct relevance to the community; (4) the audience is motivated to interact in a direct manner during or after the performance with the actors/facilitators.

Aesthetics of progressive theatre

A problem presenting itself again and again during the experimental application of theatre to rural development and adult education was to find a balance between

Box 1.2 Augusto Boal (b. Rio de Janeiro, 1931)

In his fascination and eagerness to see the audience participate actively in the theatrical event Augusto Boal developed a critical dramaturgy during the 1970s and 1980s, inspired by the aesthetics of Bertolt Brecht, the German communist playwright.

Later, influenced by Paulo Freire's critical pedagogics, Boal developed a didactics of progressive theatre techniques, experimenting with the use of theatre as a rehearsal of social interventions. He viewed theatre as a laboratory and platform for conscientisation, awareness raising and problem solving. In elaborating his first book, *Theatre of the Oppressed*, Boal combined the didactics developed by Freire and the theatre skills and techniques developed by Brecht. As a result he developed a wide range of dramatic strategies and games.

'Simultaneous dramaturgy' was such a dramatic strategy: a combination of participatory propaganda and community-generated theatre. 'Forum theatre' is another very efficient drama strategy. Here the play is performed in front of an audience twice, inviting the audience to participate directly during the second performance. Audiences now join in, change the play, argue with the characters and with each other, and generally explore the problem the play raises. Forum theatre as a process of analysis explores the limits and possibilities for action while unveiling contradictions and structures underlying everyday reality.

Analysis takes place not only through discussion but through the process of dramatisation itself, which becomes the centre of the learning experience. Invited to intervene in scenarios from everyday life – when the narrative flow is broken by posing questions and challenges to the audience – is encouraged to explore possible solutions. Spectators become actors and acting out becomes a rehearsal for action.

These dramatic games and strategies matched with another development in Central American drama, the *créación colectiva*, the collective method of drama creation as part of a wider community practice, as developed by Santiago García of the theatre group La Candelaria (Bogotá, Colombia).[6] *Créación colectiva* became a vehicle for collective examination of community and national concerns. In addition, an educational tool was created for effective community building as a partial response to these concerns.

A more recent development in Boal's work is what he calls Legislative Theatre. In 1993–6 Boal was *vereador* (Member of the City Council) for the Workers' Party in Rio de Janeiro. In this period he experimented with theatre within the political system as a means to try to create a truer form of democracy. Not accepting that the elector is a mere spectator of the actions of the parliamentarian, he creates space for the electors to present their own opinions, discuss the issues and introduce counter-arguments. In this way the active involvement of people in street performances resulted in the acceptance of a dozen new laws by the City Council.

the social and the artistic criteria for this kind of theatre. The emotional impact of a TfD playlet, based on an existing socially relevant theme, was most often felt to be more important than the artistic criteria.

During the 1970s Boal developed a pedagogy of popular theatre or community theatre, partially inspired by the intellectual heritage of Bertolt Brecht (1898–1956), who developed an aesthetics of 'progressive' theatre techniques while experimenting with the use of non-realistic theatre devices and the so-called 'alienation effects'. This served to keep the public from identifying themselves too much with the characters and succumbing to the dream effect of the conventional narrative: this was Brecht's way of questioning his own society. These new storytelling techniques, the 'modern' form of narrative art that Brecht was seeking, belonged to the historic oral tradition in many a community outside the North Atlantic cultural sphere of influence.

Boal explored areas Brecht had not touched. The former regards the making of theatre as a laboratory situation in which the participants can prepare themselves by means of theatre games to deal with future social interventions within the community or within the society as a whole. In this didactic approach the results are less important than the process.

Box 1.3 Bertolt Brecht

In the 1920s and 1930s Bertolt Brecht developed his main ideas about 'epic drama' (and theatre) as opposed to Aristotelian drama. The latter aimed at the effect of catharsis in the spectator, the freeing of emotions of fear and compassion, but for Brecht this was not the right effect to strive for in the capitalist context of his time. Instead, he wanted a form of drama and theatre that would stimulate an increased sense of political awareness in the mind of the spectator of his own situation in society (amidst recession, unemployment and rising fascism). The focus shifted from involvement to critical distance.

The epic techniques with which Brecht wanted to create an alienation effect, by placing the world of the characters on stage at a distance that alienated them from the spectators' world, were derived from different disciplines and times. These sources could vary from the theatre of Shakespeare to modern pantomime, cabaret, the circus or the acting principles of Indian or Chinese theatre. This all resulted in a play and performance structure with frequent and short sequences, quick changes of location, time or action, the use of songs and very simple set pieces, and an 'epic' acting style in which the actor is aware of the audience (speaking directly to them) instead of 'forgetting' them as is the case in 'fourth wall' theatre.

Brecht's ideas and techniques are still among the most influential ones whenever discussion focuses on the tools and possibilities of theatre from the perspective of desire for social change in today's world.

The criticism which the didactic ideas of both Brecht and Boal received during the 1980s was mostly aimed at the concept of theatre as a 'model' of social reality, a model with which you can experiment. Van der Jagt (1987a: 4; 1987b: 32) remarks quite rightly that this reality is of a much more intricate nature than the model would lead one to suspect. According to van der Jagt, a second criticism is Boal's failure to systematise his didactic approach into a consistent theatre pedagogy. The question, however, is whether one can hold this against Boal, who was in the first place a theatre maker, and not a pedagogue.

For many a critic in the North Atlantic world towards the end of the twentieth century, Brecht's and Boal's ideas were no longer valid. Yet we come across their ideas in the curricula of theatre schools in developing countries, especially those directed at the education of specialised teachers in people's theatre and community theatre contexts. This is not surprising: first, non-psychological realistic acting techniques, such as those Brecht advocated, already formed part of the local theatre traditions; second, Boal did indeed offer several accessible acting and dramatic forms useful to the making of participatory theatre.

Pioneers in TfD

TfD, or popular theatre as it was called during the 1970s, was first experimented with in Botswana, for instance, in performances that included puppets, songs and dances. The initial experiment was known as 'Laedza Batanani': an attempt to use drama and other performance forms, combined with discussion, as a vehicle for community education. The idea was to use the drawing power of theatre to bring community members together, and to focus on key local issues raised in the drama. One of the pioneers was Ross Kidd, a Canadian by birth. This contextualises the 'pre-history' of TfD, fostered at the time by university lecturers such as Kidd. Extensive documentation of the Botswana initiatives and Kidd's efforts to make contact with theatre workers in neighbouring countries meant that 'popular theatre' was soon copied and adapted by other countries in the southern, eastern and western[7] African regions.

Most initiatives at that time can be found at university level. Students took theatre courses in which they attempted to work closely with the population in mapping out local experiences of social inequality. The didactic format was the workshop. The ice-breaking games and simulation and role-play models were derived from Theatre in Education (TIE) and the revolutionary dramaturgy Augusto Boal had developed, stimulating optimal participation by local people as well as the students and other workshop contributors.

The enthusiasm of expatriate lecturers such as Kidd made African universities the site of experiments with these forms of theatre. The work in Botswana drew Michael Etherton's attention. He was affiliated with the University of Zambia (UNZA) in Lusaka and brought his expertise to a later academic post at the Ahmadu Bello University (Zaria, Nigeria), further developing his TfD experience there. In that same period David Kerr[8] initiated similar TfD experiments in Malawi.

These expatriates – now no longer directly involved in theatre – collaborated with indigenous theatre workers such as Dickson Mwansa, Mapopa Mtonga, Steve Abah, Stephen Chifunyisé, Daniel Labonne and Ngugi Wa Mirii. Together they strove to unite experiences gained in various countries.[9] As well as dedicating themselves to setting up various African networks, they also worked hard to organise national and international meetings, and to demand international attention for TfD as an instrument for development support communication in Africa.

Kidd returned to Canada continuing his studies in adult education at the University of Toronto in 1978. During his journey home he travelled through Africa and Asia making contact with local popular theatre workers. The following year Kidd travelled the Caribbean and Central America. His objective was to learn from theatre workers in other parts of the world how they applied theatre for participatory development. The results were published in his PhD thesis on TfD. The best way to study 'best practices' at that time was to combine studies with practical work in this field. Through the International Council for Adult Education, Kidd helped organise a series of training workshops on TfD in Canada as well as Bangladesh, Cameroon, the Eastern Caribbean, Nigeria, Zambia and Zimbabwe. This gave him ample opportunities to visit many of the emerging TfD projects in the field.

Meticulously networking, publishing and inspiring people, Kidd wrote a report after each trip, which often contained a combination of analysis and lively description. He was thus able to write about initiatives by PETA (the Philippines), by Proshika and other groups (Bangladesh), by several theatre groups in India, and by theatre practitioners such as Ngugi wa Mirii and Ngugi wa Thiong'o (Kenya), Raul Leis[10] (Panama) and Michael Etherton (first in Zambia and later in Nigeria). With seemingly inexhaustible energy he convinced many bilateral donor agencies of the importance of bringing culture into the field of development. This triggered several international expert meetings and conferences during the 1980s and 1990s, as well as a number of workshops at a more national level, which retrospectively made a very important networked impact.

International networking and collaboration

At the end of the 1970s, Ross Kidd, then closely linked to the research unit of the International Council of Adult Education (ICAE) and Nat Colletta of the World Bank, took the initiative by promoting the first international seminar on 'The Use of Indigenous Social Structures and Traditional Media in Non-formal Education and Development', organised by the German Foundation for International Development (DSE)[11] and ICAE in Berlin in 1980. The seminar dealt with the use of popular culture and (performing) arts as small-scale media in development support communication activities. Two subjects were discussed: the role of indigenous institutions in processes of social change; and the role of performing arts in both mass campaigns and non-formal education projects at community level.

Table 1.1 A selection of international conferences and workshop seminars on Theatre for Development

Year	Country	Place	Title of conference
1980	Germany	Berlin	International Seminar on 'The Use of Indigenous Social Structures and Traditional Media in Non-formal Education and Development', 5–12 November (Berlin), organised by the German Foundation for International Development (DSE) and the International Council for Adult Education (ICAE).
1982	Nigeria	Kaduna	'First Benue International Popular Theatre Workshop for Development', Gboko (Benue State, Nigeria), 28 December–9 January, organised by the Benue Council for Arts and Culture (Harding, 1999).
1983	Bangladesh	Dhaka /Koitta	'Popular Theatre Dialogue', 4–14 February, organised by the International Council of Adult Education (ICAE).
1983	Zimbabwe	Harare	'Consultative Conference on African Theatre', University of Harare, 3–5 September. Held under the auspices of UNESCO, the conference gave birth to the Union of African Performing Artists (UAPA), a pan-African organisation.
1988	Mauritius		Africa Symposium Workshop (AFSYMWORK), 15–29 October, organised by the International Theatre Institute (ITI) and the International Amateur Theatre Association (IATA).
1991	Namibia	Windhoek /Rehoboth	International Popular Theatre Workshop, 1–14 August, organised by the International Council of Adult Education (ICAE) and the African Council of Adult Education (ALAE).
1998	Kenya	Kisumu	3rd IDEA World Congress of Drama/Theatre and Education, 9–19 July, organised by the Kenya Drama/Theatre and Education Association (KDEA).

With the financial support of the DSE some forty international experts in that field were brought together. They came from all continents and from different working contexts, and included practitioners, researchers, non-formal educators, development communicators, senior civil servants and grassroots workers.

After this seminar the DSE published one of the first readers on this subject, *Tradition for Development* (edited by Kidd and Colletta). Printed in a limited edition, it became a collectors' item. Moreover, the intercontinental networking began in earnest. Plans were made for more practical follow-up workshops to be organised in 'the field': developing countries.

Soon various national and regional seminars were organised (see Table 1.1), sited in 'the field', which were of a much more practical nature. In addition, a start was made with national associations and formal networks. Well known from the 1970s are the Philippine Educational Theatre Association (PETA)[12] and the Movimiento de Expresión Campesino Artística (MECATE), Nicaragua. From the early 1980s onwards, several national popular theatre associations (networks) were added: the Zimbabwe Association for Community Theatres (ZACT), the Zambian National Theatre Arts Association (ZANTAA), the People's Educational Theatre (PET) association in Swaziland, and the Kenya Drama/Theatre and Education Association (KDEA). These associations and their networks organised regular meetings. At the global level, attempts have been made to establish a network of networks.

International Popular Theatre Alliance (IPTA)

In 1983 Ross Kidd and Ahmed Faruque of Proshika succeeded in organising an international popular theatre meeting in Koitta, a small Hindu village located forty miles to the North of Dhaka, the capital of Bangladesh.

Significantly, this International Popular Theatre Dialogue was opened not by the Minister of Culture or Education, but by a landless labourer from a local theatre group. Some seventy drama teachers, development practitioners and actors from all over the world assembled. The participants from Bangladesh were part-time actors and actresses belonging to the Aranyak theatre group, Proshika animators and peasants running theatre groups in their own villages and working in small-scale and, therefore, inexpensive awareness-raising projects.

The foreigners were all TfD practitioners from Africa, Asia, Canada and the Caribbean islands. All were involved in progressive and politically oriented popular theatre. There was ample opportunity, therefore, to fill a dozen days with a lively exchange of ideas, experiences and practices.

One of the results of this meeting was the foundation of the International Popular Theatre Alliance (IPTA):[13] an informal network of popular theatre practitioners that published a newsletter and moved its office every three years. In 1984 the Asian region was willing to host and administrate the network until 1987. Its office was located at the Philippine Educational Theatre Association (PETA). This initiative received sympathy and modest support from the International Council of Adult Education (ICAE), Canada.

The Philippines-based secretariat focused on a permanent exchange of information and experience by means of the *International Popular Theatre Newsletter*, conferences and seminars. It was the policy of the Alliance to promote the exchange of teachers and animators working in the field of popular theatre in the various regions. At that time, during the first half of the 1980s, people involved in producing action-oriented theatre were constantly at risk of being imprisoned or exiled on political grounds. Consequently the IPTA secretariat played an active part in presenting political petitions and declarations of solidarity.

In 1991 an International Popular Theatre Workshop took place in Rehoboth, a small village 80 kilometres South of Windhoek (Namibia). The first objective of this drama meeting was to train the Namibian cultural workers engaged in the establishment of community theatre at the basis of society. The participants consisted of some forty Namibian and thirty-five foreign guests. This event also received technical assistance from the International Council for Adult Education (ICAE), and was organised in close cooperation with the government of Namibia.[14]

The International Drama/Theatre and Education Association (IDEA)

Parallel to these IPTA activities drama teachers took an initiative to build up an international network. This resulted in the International Drama/Theatre and Education Association (IDEA), which was formally registered in Portugal (1992) at the first IDEA World Congress, held in Porto. In 1994 it became a fully constituted international organisation.[15]

The work of this association reflects a clear social as well as artistic aim. Three purposes have bound IDEA's activities together. First, the association has aimed to address the role of theatre and drama in establishing personal, cultural and social identity. Second, it has sought to provide a space for dialogue and for personal and social transformation. Finally, in a world containing many forms of exclusion, violence and threat, IDEA has promoted drama/theatre as a powerful tool for educators working towards peace. It therefore addresses the cultural, artistic and educational needs of people, particularly children and youngsters. For example, IDEA has endorsed anti-violence projects in such devastated areas as the Sudan and South-Eastern Europe.

IDEA has developed into an international forum for drama and theatre educators and other theatre-related practitioners who use drama and theatre as part of a dynamic, relevant, contemporary education. At present IDEA comprises fifty associations in over sixty countries on five continents. Its main objectives are:

1 to offer a forum for meeting and discussion to individual persons, groups and institutions throughout the world who are working and campaigning for the universal right to arts education and in particular for the place of drama/theatre in the education of each person;

2 to facilitate international communication and dissemination of information through publications and the organisation of seminars, workshops, symposia and conferences on subjects relevant to drama/theatre and education;

3 to support the development of research into the theory and practice of drama/ theatre and education, particularly through the dissemination of research reports within the international community;

4 to promote and encourage regional, national and international initiatives consistent with these objectives by facilitating the exchange of drama/theatre observers, practitioners and educators.

In 1998 the Kenya Drama/Theatre and Education Association (KDEA) organised the IDEA World Congress in Kisumu. During this conference TfD in Africa received special attention.

Documenting experiences

The bulk of TfD publications were published between the mid-1970s and the mid-1990s, when the flow somewhat abated. As with all new subjects the first publications – during the 1960s – consisted of bland literature, hand-outs, conference papers, and reports on national and regional meetings. Soon afterwards the first articles appeared in magazines and professional journals. These texts were rather descriptive in nature and were presented as case study materials on local experiences or as national surveys on TfD workshops.

During the 1970s and up to the mid-1980s little was published on the methodology of the TfD approach, with the exception of work by Ross Kidd (Botswana) and Raul Leis (Panama), who sought to integrate TfD in adult education. At this time, it should be noted, Augusto Boal was writing about drama as a social action strategy for cultural activists, while the publications of the Philippine Educational Theatre Association (PETA) were also becoming available: these were much more in line with Theatre in Education (TIE) thinking.[16]

The first *books* on the subject of TfD appeared between the late 1980s and the mid-1990s. Most described experiences at national and regional level, dealing with TfD in India or sub-Saharan Africa. Typically, they assembled texts previously published in magazines and journals.

Some authors (Breitinger, Etherton, Kerr, Plastow, Ricard) placed TfD within a postcolonial literary tradition. They studied the literary value of drama texts produced by TfD as part of popular and contemporary theatre history in various parts of Africa. So far, little has been published on the methodology of TfD specifically from the perspective of development studies.

During the 1990s several new series of studies of TfD appeared. Its early history became the subject of the research undertaken by David Kerr and Lee Dale Byam, both of whom made detailed presentations of TfD's early days, focusing especially on sub-Saharan Africa. On the other hand, a series of country-specific studies also appeared: Francis Harding on TfD in Nigeria, Jane Plastow on Eritrea, Lee Dale Byam on Zimbabwe, Zakes Mda on Lesotho, Penina Muhando Mlama on Tanzania and Christopher Kamlongera on Malawi. Most are descriptive in nature: they relate TfD's contemporary history and deal with the textual contents of the plays, the context of workshops and performances, TfD experiences as related to the development of literary drama, and the role TfD has played in the context of 'culture and development' in those specific countries.

The Centre for the Study of Education in Developing Countries (CESO, The Hague) set up a modest library and documentation collection on TfD books, papers and 'grey literature' during the 1980s and 1990s. This collection has been moved to the library of King Alfred's College in Winchester, United Kingdom. Since the late 1990s the College has offered an MA in TfD.

Those interested in learning how TfD live performances measure up to theatrical and/or literary standards may be interested by the International Theatre Festival for Development (FITD) – a biennial event organised by the Atelier-Théâtre Burkinabè (ATB)[17] in Burkina Faso since 1988. Here, performers are brought together with the aim of stimulating a subregional and eventually worldwide cooperation to promote TfD. In 1998, more than 88 groups from 25 countries attended. They presented TfD performances and plays on topics such as teenage pregnancy, female circumcision, family planning and politics.

Audio-visual registration of TfD experiences (performances and workshops) has been poor. Some edited audio-visual material exists: on 'community theatre' (produced by Eugène van Erven); on TfD as used in Kenya (some instructive videos by Loukie Levert); or on Boal techniques as used in Brazil (material recorded by A Resource for Theatre in Participating Development – ARTPAD). The collection, nonetheless, is as yet quite modest. As the videos on early experiences with TfD have become so rare, there is some urgency to collect these tapes and preserve their contents.

Conclusion

NGOs and institutions for adult education have been the prime developers of the idea of using performing arts as popular media in non-formal education. At university level, departments of adult education carried out experiments in rural development that integrated the performing arts in non-formal educational activities such as literacy programmes, community development and adult education. As a result, according to Mda (1993: 46), adult educators and development workers came together to explore development issues, create dramas as 'codes' and facilitate analysis and discussion with spectators/participants at community level.

During the 1960s and 1970s target audiences were approached by adult educators and development practitioners in order to use creative and cultural assets (such as applied drama methods) to support local communities in becoming aware of and changing the poor and oppressed living situations. Initially this approach was welcomed by the political and cultural élite of many young African nations in an attempt to stimulate an active participation of the people in the arts.

This progressive view did not receive political support from all regimes, however. In some countries social action to improve the position of the oppressed within the community was obstructed. In Africa, for instance, this resulted in the imposition of censorship on 'popular theatre' by one-party governments and dictatorial regimes during the postcolonial period – the best-known example being the Kenyan government's reaction to performances at the Kamiriithu Community Education and Cultural Centre in 1977.[18]

After TfD's initial success, governmental and multilateral organisations have come to see theatre as a relatively inexpensive educational tool involving local people as performers. It seems to avoid the problem of illiteracy by using the language of the people, performs free of charge in public places, and deals with local problems and situations with which everyone can identify. This, however, is a simplified view. To make TfD successful in 'the field' takes more.

During the 1980s TfD was used as an instrument to contribute to all kinds of local problem-solving processes. Ultimately, however, it was felt that the way to solve problems successfully was obstructed by undemocratic political structures which had to be changed first. After 1989 new democratic political structures seemed to open the way forward, but since then political barriers have been replaced by economic ones.

Although much has happened in the world over the last forty years with regard to the organisation of TfD, a clear framework and direction for the future seem to be lacking. It is as if the various theatre groups and networks share a certain collective political orientation and commitment, while their practical activities and development of concepts differ considerably.

2

The Context in Which TfD has Developed*

'According to the contemporary development discourse, the recipient should have ownership of the programme in order to enhance programme success.' (Seppälä and Vainio-Mattila, 2000: 38)

'Culture can be a source of rich and sustainable development or a brake on change, an obstacle and a source of division.' (Matarasso, 2001: 9)

How far can the rise of TfD be explained by changes in development approaches and cultural policies over the last decades? Certainly TfD has been an instrument of social change within the framework of development approaches. Moreover, TfD itself is a cultural expression, a means of communication and a way of reinforcing and perpetuating culture. As such, it has influenced development and cultural policies, and policy developments have recognised the role of the arts in society and its use for development purposes.

Here I describe recent changes in development approaches and cultural policies, including their effect on the role of theatre in society and development processes. In general, development approaches have evolved from small-scale, specific, problem-solving interventions into broad support programmes to improve a country's socio-economic sector. The 'ownership' of these interventions – who is responsible for the projects and their results – has also changed. In the past projects were designed and executed *for* the beneficiaries, while now the beneficiaries play a much greater role in the planning and implementation of interventions.

Cultural policies around the world show a great variety: in some places culture is seen as a rather static component of social life, while in others it is regarded as an important factor in social survival strategies. Cultural policies tend to be designed to conserve and nurture cultural expressions, whereas development

---

* Essays in Part II which relate to the contents of this chapter are:
   Chapter 7 Development support modalities and planning processes
   Chapter 11 The importance of art education

workers and donor agencies have developed approaches that tap cultural resources for development and conflict resolution purposes. Cultural policies refer to their objectives as 'cultural development', while development policies speak of 'culture and development'.

Trends in development approaches

The collapse of the USSR and the demise of twentieth century socialism had a huge impact on the theory, practices and funding of 'development cooperation'. It initiated a global tendency at the macroeconomic level to strive for a transition from a state-controlled towards a market-controlled economy. As a consequence the following major shifts in development support modalities – with clear implications for the cultural sector – took place.

1 The end of the Cold War shifted the relative balance of financial support from explicitly political and military activities to support for processes of conflict prevention, peacekeeping, reconciliation, rebuilding nations and poverty alleviation or relief work. War zones such as the Balkans, the Caucasus and the Horn of Africa (Eritrea, Ethiopia and Somalia) received special attention.

2 Bilateral donors now tend to support specific regions or countries. Such donors, especially in Europe, have decreased the number of countries they support. New funding programmes were initiated especially to help Central and Eastern European states to rebuild their countries and to enable them to become (associated) members of the European Union (EU) in due course. Bilateral donors and the EU concentrated on regions such as MERCOSUR,[19] the Pacific Rim, South and Central Asia and sub-Saharan Africa.

3 There is less incidental project support and more programmes of structural, long-term and sector-wide support (this new emphasis is also known as the Sector-Wide Approach or SWAp).

Many international organisations, national governments and non-governmental organisations in the North and South have been actively involved in shaping and changing past and present development support policies.

Development

Thinking in terms of 'development' has a history originating in the Euro-American Enlightenment. The product of this ideology is a grand narrative – especially strong in the field of development studies during the 1950s and early 1960s – that invested modernisation with great expectations.

One might think of development as an inclusive process involving qualitative and structural change and resulting in the improvement of the quality of life of the community as a whole. Or, following Inayatullah (1967:102), one might regard development as a process in which society (1) gains increasing control over the environment; (2) achieves increasing control over its own political fate; and (3) offers its members increasing control over themselves.

Whatever definition is opted for,[20] over the past forty years 'development' was primarily concerned with economic growth, technological progress and social prosperity. The importance of culture often received little attention. The central objective of development cooperation was and still is the pursuit of structural poverty alleviation though economic processes.

In the late 1970s the World Bank and the International Monetary Fund (IMF) introduced Structural Adjustment Programmes (SAPs) for many developing countries in order to renegotiate their debts. The majority of these reforms propagated decentralisation. The underlying hypothesis of those reforms was that by transferring responsibilities and resources to smaller administrative and political units, the services transferred would become more responsive to the citizens. It was hoped that in the end these SAPs would call for some kind of guarantee of 'good governance' and 'sustainable development' by decentralising and outsourcing public services formerly monopolised by the national government.

At a ministerial level, decentralisation implies a shift from supervision to monitoring, from control to coaching and quality assurance, from implementing at a central level to providing opportunities for others to implement at local levels. This applies to all social sectors, including basic education (formal as well as non-formal), literacy training, health services and sanitation. It applies to the cultural sector as well.

Conventional and participatory models of development

In development cooperation a distinction is made between conventional top-down and more recent bottom-up models of planning and managing of development activities. The top-down model is characteristic of private enterprise and state regimes working along centralised and hierarchical government principles. Planners and decision makers at the top of the hierarchy identify and develop plans for projects and programmes for the beneficiaries of these projects and programmes. The beneficiaries may be consulted during the identification process. In general, however, they are not involved in decision making, nor do they carry large responsibilities in the implementation of the projects or programmes. They are expected to cooperate and contribute when required and to maintain the project's results after its implementation.

From the 1970s onwards the development models used by government agencies supported by donors came under heavy fire, especially from development practitioners working under the aegis of NGOs and university departments. Challenging the technocratic approach to development cooperation, they started small-scale field pilots to prove that a participatory way of working might be more effective than the conventional approaches featuring top-down social engineering. This bottom-up form of participatory planning and management involved the beneficiaries as primary stakeholders in the planning of their own development from the first step onwards. This created stakeholder ownership of the planned activities. It also increased the likelihood that they would not only take part in the

Table 2.1 Comparing conventional and participatory development models

	Conventional approaches	**Participatory approaches**
Problem solving	Recipe approach: providing standard 'recipe' solutions to problems, identified by an outside agency and developed by an expert coming from outside the community	Partnership approach: developing solutions together by accepting and appreciating all parties involved for contributing their specific expertise to a common solution
Focus	Top-down: project-centred or subject-centred; individual changes lead to job improvement	Bottom-up: community centred; initiatives developed by the participants themselves, from their point of view; collective reflection and actions lead to solution(s) to identified problems
Way of communicating	One-way (monologue)	Dialogue
Pedagogical principles	Learning by heart: learning individuals are given knowledge (and skills) and are expected to change their behaviour in due course	Learning by doing: practical training to provide opportunities to the participants to change their own situation
Relation between trainer and trainee	Trainer-centred: trainer teaches and learners learn	Learner-centred: learners identify learning needs, set goals and learn for themselves; the educator is a facilitator of the process

implementation of these activities but also feel responsible for sustaining the results afterwards.

Experiments with the bottom-up model at community level were brought together under the common denominator of 'participatory development', an alternative to the old politics of 'conventional development'. Participatory development required locally emerging and fluctuating processes of development that responded flexibly to the changing needs and priorities of local community or the primary stakeholders. Instruments were developed – among them participatory training and participatory research methods – enabling stakeholders to identify needs and priorities.

What all these participatory methods have in common is that the primary stakeholders have a say in designing and implementing their own development (programmes). Participatory methods were introduced in every sector (including education, culture, health and agriculture) and at each level of programme implementation (planning and design, decision making, implementation and evaluation) (Belisle, Bhog and Jung, 1997: 181).

From this interaction, the planners learned how to handle unexpected side-effects of development interventions by opting for flexible planning models that could be adjusted without having to start from scratch again. Practitioners in the field discovered how planning models may help to turn pilot projects into sustainable and long-term initiatives that can be taken over by the communities themselves as self-supporting components fully integrated within a wider grid of regional and national development plans.

Top-down and bottom-up models of development differ strongly in philosophy, in strategy and process. They may serve the same overall objectives but use different roads to realise them. The models differ in the way problems and needs are identified and activities are carried out and managed. The strategies and instruments characterising both models are further explained in Chapter 7. TfD clearly falls into the category of participatory approaches as it is aimed at achieving community participation, empowerment and learning by doing. This will be discussed further in Chapter 3.

At the start of the twenty-first century, both these development models continue to exist in parallel, without being competitive. After three decades of experience, practitioners of both approaches recognise and accept the strengths and weaknesses of both models. Experiments are being carried out using strict planning instruments parallel to participatory techniques in order to achieve tailor-made medium- and long-term action plans at community as well as at national level.

Partners in development

During the 1970s and early 1980s donor agencies were predominantly the implementers of projects. Interventions were generally, though not always, small-scale ones. Development was still viewed by many as essentially an economic rather than a social issue. Over the years, the involvement and interaction of different actors or parties in processes of development, and their influence on international policies, have significantly increased. Many organisations, belonging neither to the public nor to the private sector, have been called into being by motivated civilians wishing to contribute to a just society, not only in their own country but also in developing countries. It is because these organisations are financed and managed neither by state officials nor by commercial agencies, but by civilians, that this 'third sector' has also been referred to as 'civil society'.

Together with 'state' and 'market', 'civil society' is one of the three domains engaged in the making of democratic society. In that sense, civil society is a historically evolved sphere of individual rights, freedoms and voluntary associations whose politically undisturbed competition with each other in the pursuit of their respective concerns, interests, preferences and intentions is guaranteed by a public institution called the state (Council of Europe, 1997: 150).

Early forerunners of the third sector are religious custodian organisations such as the (local) church, the mosque or the temple. These institutions rendered their services to the local community or society at large in terms of charity and education. Other examples are organisations set up by labour unions or political parties to train their cadres and to offer services to their members. At present, human rights and environmental groups contribute to the emergence of a pluralist civil society.

The public, private and third sectors invest substantial financial resources into development processes through a variety of channels: intermediate organisations such as official bilateral or multilateral donor organisations, development banks, or direct partnerships with counterpart organisations in the South. Whatever legal form these organisations take, they are commonly referred to as non-governmental organisations (NGOs) in order to distinguish them from governmental organisations (GOs), non-profit organisations (NPOs) and private enterprise.

It has come to be accepted in development policy that strengthening civil society is an essential prerequisite for social cohesion and sustainable development. An indicator of social cohesion is the democratic sharing of power, meaning the ability to act and the ability to act on the actions of others. Therefore, culture-oriented organisations forming part of civil society are indirectly involved in the practical implementation of political and economic development strategies.

Nowadays 'state', 'market' and 'civil society' are considered to be partners in development efforts. The partnership concept reveals the political realities within which development support is conceived and nurtured. The term 'partnership' implies that groups when coming together carry with them their own abilities, strengths and constraints. Moreover, it implies that institutions, organisations and individuals have different human, material and financial resources and sources of power which can be pooled in order to confront the complex realities of poor and marginalised groups. Partners are considered to be able to recognise differences and inequalities in their respective competencies, but they build upon each partner's strength to achieve a successful partnership. This is considered to be the added value of the partnership.

In this framework, the community should also play a part. The poor community in a developing country may be regarded as the beneficiary of development support, but the support will not be effective if the community is not asked to share responsibility for the process and does not contribute to its abilities. The community should be a partner in the process aiming at uplifting its welfare.[21]

During the 1970s the first 'pilots' started with an interventionist development approach referred to as 'community development'. On the one hand community development consists of extension work (such as preventive health care), which is quite message-oriented; and, on the other hand, of awareness raising, which is more process-oriented (local leadership training, for example). Community development leading to community organisation is a very powerful tool if used in the right way.

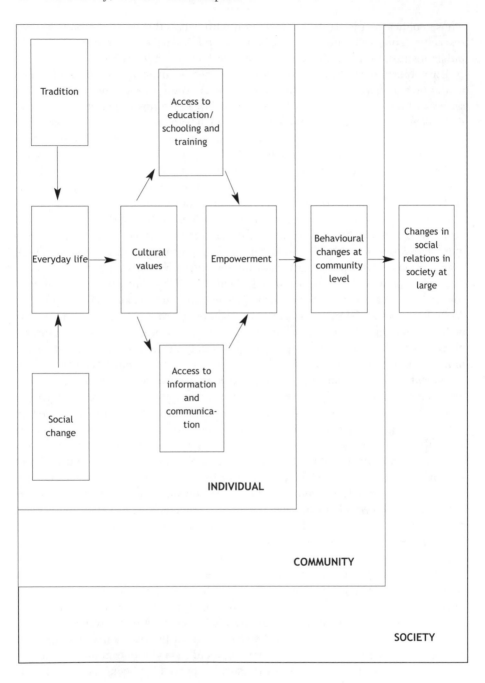

Figure 2.1 Schematic links between education, communication, empowerment and behavioural change

Although substantial amounts of funds are being budgeted for the upliftment and development of local communities, members of these communities are still rarely consulted in development planning and usually have no active role in the implementation of development activities. In the eyes of the mainstream investors the vast majority of the poor lack literacy skills and have no organisational structures to represent their interests. Isolated, under-educated and often dependent on local élites, they lack the means to win greater access to resources and markets, or to prevent the imposition of unworkable programmes or technologies.

Development, culture and the arts

Culture: a matter of definition

Culture was seen as a factor of resistance, a formidable opponent to change, during the 1950s. The 'traditional way of life' was an obstacle to be overcome by any possible means if one wished to reap the fruits of modernity: wealth, health and respect in an ever-widening circle of developed nations.

This view of culture as an obstacle to social change and development slowly evolved into its opposite. Nowadays it is generally accepted that culture offers an enabling environment to development. Because the way of life of a community is largely determined by cultural factors, it is not possible to intervene in its development without taking the cultural beliefs and practices of the community into account (Gould, 2001: 71).

From the 1990s onwards, instigated by drastic political changes, more dynamic and problem-focused definitions of 'culture' have been preferred: cultures are seen as human survival programmes '(re)developed' time and again responding to continuous changing situations. In these definitions, culture is considered as a 'life support system', a form of 'human capital'[22] that (1) affects people's capacity to deal with the challenges of everyday life; and (2) provides a given group with mechanisms of self-regulation to react to sudden changes in their social and physical environment.

Nowadays, culture is seen as a resource.

In 1992, the Council of Europe (1997) provided one all-embracing definition of culture: at its most extensive, culture encompasses the totality of a community's learned experience as reflected in its conventions and values – economic, legal, political, religious, moral, familial, technological, scientific and aesthetic. In view of the very general nature of this definition Everitt proposes a further distinction between A, B and C cultures.[23] He takes the anthropological definition of culture used in the MONDIACULT Declaration (Mexico City, 1982) as A culture: 'In its widest sense, culture may now be said to be the whole complex of distinctive spiritual, material, intellectual and emotional features of a society or a social group, encompassing, in addition to art and literature, lifestyles, ways of living together, value systems, traditions and beliefs.'

B culture is described by means of the comprehensive definition of the arts which appears in Public Law 209 of the 89th United States Congress: 'The term "the arts" includes, but is not limited to, music (instrumental and vocal), dance, drama, folk art, creative writing, architecture and allied fields, painting, sculpture, photography, graphic and craft arts, industrial design, costume and fashion design, motion pictures, television, radio, tape and sound recording, the arts related to the presentations, performance, execution, and exhibition of such major art forms, and the study and application of the arts to the human environment.'

C culture refers to the 'high arts', those works of art which acquaint the public with the best that has been known and said in the world, and thus with the history of the human spirit. C culture includes masterpieces and best practices as collected and saved for mankind, as in museums.

It is beyond serious argument that popular culture (B culture) and even the high arts (C culture) usefully contribute to societal values in general (A culture) and to the institutions expressing them.

Cultural identity

People sharing the same culture also share a common identity. They feel they belong to a group and live according to its mores. Most contemporary societies in the South as well as in the North are multi-ethnic, enclosing within their borders a larger number of cultures. European society has a multicultural character. The same applies to North America. Several ethnic groups belong to a cultural majority and others to cultural minorities. According to Dors (1990: 28) ethnic minorities are groups not in a dominant position, socio-economically and politically speaking. At the start of the 1990s, about one hundred and sixty nation states housed some ten thousand societies in the world, each with its own distinct cultural identity.

In this context cultural identity refers to an articulated set of values, world views, and presuppositions held by a local population or a nation at large, most clearly expressed in tangible and intangible cultural products.[24] In the first case, we speak of a local or ethnic cultural identity. In the second, we speak of a national identity. In a pluralistic society, within the boundaries of the state, the local cultural identity is usually under pressure from the national cultural identity.

From this definition, it appears that 'identity' brings people together and separates or distinguishes groups of people. After all, individuals, groups, societies or nations all take their identities by distinguishing themselves from *others*'. This difference between people can be felt when they experience the contrast between their cultural ideals and the cultural reality they live in. In spite of national boundaries separating them, people still strive to unite as one.

Generally speaking, three indicators are used to establish the existence of a cultural identity: a common language, moral values and political organisation. People usually feel strengthened in their group identity if group members speak the same language while sharing the same moral values and a common political organisation. Language, values and political organisation have been embedded in a shared cultural heritage, or a shared past, through history, local oral tradition and cultural practices (including the performing arts). The search for identity means a search both backwards into what has been, and forwards to what might come.

Despite the aforementioned conflicting social forces, the individual has a choice of different cultural identities. The individual may identify with fellow group members on the basis of very general or highly specific characteristics: sex, education, age, sports, leisure activities, etcetera. He or she may also identify with people who regularly meet in the church, parish, youth club, neighbourhood or school or during events such as conferences, dances or music classes.

Cultural change

Cultures are certainly not immortal. As shared complexes of values, norms, attitudes, beliefs and customs, cultures are subject to change. For that reason traditions have been invented as a human response to change. By keeping up (and thus preserving) traditions people try to call a halt to change.

Since the introduction and general acceptance of modern thought in Western society, however, change has been accepted as the basis, the essential quality and the dynamo of modernism. Modern thought continuously starts (or continues by re-starting) from a critical deconstruction of the immediate past which, in fact, calls for the invention and *reinvention* of the past (in terms of traditions, for example). The past has to make sense in an ever-changing present. This generates a continuous 'identity crisis' as a chronic condition, afflicting nations as well as individuals. A permanent area of tension is created between the danger of losing, distorting and expropriating traditional forms of cultural expression and the need to create new forms.

Although social change is an ongoing process, it is sometimes triggered by outside interventions, which may take place casually and/or intentionally. Interventions of a more incidental nature are made up of all kinds of 'spontaneous' meetings or confrontations leading to cultural (ex)changes. Outside interventions launched on purpose are made up of all kinds of political interventions (including violent oppression) and military interventions (war). These interventions are quite destructive in nature. Other outside interventions are explicitly focused on innovation. Development interventions are launched with the intention of changing the culture of the community by means of innovation, implying that innovation and intervention are two variables in processes of social change.[25] This leaves us with two modalities of social change: (1) innovation without intervention and (2) innovation through intervention. The first kind of innovation evolves when some traditions or cultural expressions disappear because they no longer fulfil the needs of society. Others are creatively changed and adjusted to technological and commercial challenges. Or to a new public, including tourists and visiting political and diplomatic dignitaries. Sometimes an entire genre of cultural expression no longer represents that living reality, necessitating *invention* of new meanings and forms of expression to suit the new situation (Kleymeyer, 1993: 200).

The second kind of innovation takes place continuously by means of education, which transmits societal values and behavioural patterns in order to maintain the existing social organisation. Yet, there is a continuous tension between the conservative and the innovative nature of education because at the same time education contributes to streamlining social change. However, such processes of change do not come about in a vacuum but are fed by what is going on within society at large.

The same contradictory powers are at work in culture: (1) it preserves elements from the past while also acting as a creative force; and (2) it copes with future problem solving and change. However, subtle changes in time are not discussed when people choose to think that cultural traditions are passing unchanged from one generation to the next. In order to preserve traditions, the living have often transformed them, because culture has to change constantly if it is to remain meaningful to the living.

Table 2.2 Modalities of social change

	Preservation/conservation	**Innovation**
Intervention	Education/Heritage/ Archives	Outside development initiatives
Non-intervention	Regular maintenance	Endogenous development

Culture and development versus cultural development

The intricate relation between culture, identity, change and development has been debated at various international conferences mainly initiated by the United Nations Educational, Scientific and Cultural Organisation (UNESCO). These international meetings created the platform for an open dialogue on this issue.

One of the first initiatives was the formulation of the cultural dimension of development as an alternative to the one-sided emphasis on the economic-technological dimension. It was launched at the World Conference on Cultural Policies (MONDIACULT, Mexico City, 1982) that brought together the national ministers of culture under the auspices of UNESCO. This event provided the United Nations General Assembly with a framework to launch the UN World Decade for Cultural Development (WDCD, 1988–97), paying special attention to the cultural component of development processes and the strengthening of the cultural identity of those involved. The World Decade of Cultural Development had the following objectives: (1) to acknowledge the cultural dimension of development; (2) to enrich cultural identities; (3) to broaden participation in cultural life; and (4) to promote international cultural cooperation.

In December 1992 the independent World Commission on Culture and Development (WCCD) was founded under the presidency of Javier Pérez de Cuéllar. The UN and UNESCO had mandated this Commission to prepare a policy-oriented

Table 2.3 'Culture and development' as distinguished from 'cultural development'

	Culture and development	**Cultural development**
Aiming at	Contribution of culture to sustainable development	Promotion of participation in cultural life
Result	Means to an end	End in itself
Targeted countries	Developing and transition countries	Developed countries
Targeted audiences	Deprivileged and marginalised groups in society	Society at large (population at national level)
Scope	Local action strategies	Mainstream cultural policies
Implementers	Non-governmental organisations (NGOs)/Civil Society	Governmental organisations (GOs)
Policies	Cultural strategy as a key component in development policy	Cultural policies in general and at national level
Practicalities	Practicalities of implementing development objectives into cultural programmes and projects at community level	Practicalities of promoting and stimulating creativity and participation in cultural life in society as a whole
Heritage	Safeguard and enhance cultural heritage in so far as access to cultural heritage is part of cultural rights	Safeguard and enhance cultural heritage in general at national level
Identity	Building local identity	Building national identity

report on the interactions between culture and development, resulting in the presentation of *Our Creative Diversity* in 1995.

The original assertion of the UNESCO World Commission on Culture and Development was: culture is a holistic dimension of sustainable development. As development is about 'the widening of human opportunities and choices', culture must play a role in enabling individuals and communities to define their needs and futures according to their own traditions, values, identities and rights. Culture must be taken into account if development is planned to be sustainable.

In 1997 the Council of Europe set up a parallel initiative to the WCCD, producing *In from the Margins*, a report that was in part a follow-up to UNESCO's *Our Creative Diversity*. Although the subtitle of the Council of Europe report refers to 'culture and development', its contents are focused on 'cultural development' within the European context. The report set forth overt indications that 'culture and development' and 'cultural development' were growing apart along two lines of thought.

Another milestone in UNESCO's involvement in 'culture and development' was the Intergovernmental Conference on Cultural Policies for Development organised in close collaboration with the Swedish Government (Stockholm, 1998). This conference even went on to develop an action plan on 'cultural policies for development'.

This implied a final shift from 'culture and development', via 'cultural development' to 'cultural policies (for development)' within a European as well as a world-wide context. Table 2.3 presents a listing of some of the main differences between 'culture and development' and 'cultural development' policies.

Cultural and development policies

Due to the aforementioned world conferences on culture and development, (bilateral) donor agencies began to understand the importance of involving cultural strategies within the context of developing processes. According to Niehof (n.d.), at the start of the 1990s development policies paid keen attention to culture. Progress was made at two levels. First, culture itself had become an autonomous development activity. Artists could participate in international events. Second, the cultural dimension of development was integrated into all kinds of project activities. The concept of 'culture' proved its relevance with regard to various issues such as: (1) the socio-cultural setting within which development activities take place; (2) the ways of living and thinking within a community subjected to processes of social change; and (3) cultural manifestations which are preserved (such as heritage and patrimony), promoted (such as performing arts),[26] or exchanged (visual arts and literature) through international cooperation.

Consequently, during the first half of the 1990s most (bilateral) donor agencies within the North Atlantic region were very much in favour of 'culture and development' issues. Most policy reports even contained a special paragraph devoted to the importance of 'culture and development'.

The Canadian International Development Agency (CIDA) published a paper on 'Society, Culture and Sustainable Development' in 1991. It describes, in rather abstract terms, the anthropological concept of 'culture' as one of five elements (cultural, economic, environmental, political and social) which in an integrated way make up sustainable development.

The Netherlands' Directorate General of International Cooperation (DGIS) paid attention to the cultural dimension of development in its policy document *A World of Difference: a New Framework for Development Cooperation During the 1990s*.[27] In Dutch development policy, culture is not regarded as irrelevant or as an obstacle to development, but rather as a basis for sustainable development. In that sense – according to the report – economic and technological development cannot be seen as separate from the cultural context. Moreover, in Dutch policy, culture is not regarded as sacred or static, but as dynamic and subject to continuous change.

In 1995, the Swedish International Development Cooperation Agency (SIDA) published a report entitled *The Role of Culture in Development*. It discusses the various cultural subsectors, disciplines and institutions – such as literature, theatre, museums, dance, music, visual arts, crafts and film – that feature in South–South and North–South development cooperation. In addition, the report acknowledges the importance of supporting capacity building and institutional strengthening in the field of 'culture and development' in the South.[28] This report also deals with the role children's and young people's theatre plays, for instance, regarding reconciliation and healing processes in El Salvador, Mozambique and South Africa. Outreach programmes and training, both in community theatre and in theatre as artistic expression, should be prioritised in order to decentralise and even out an unfair distribution of theatrical activities.

Tim Butchard wrote the British Council (BC) original 'Arts and Development' paper emphasising three factors hitherto either neglected or underemphasised both by the British Council and by other cultural and donor agencies: (1) culture is the fundamental dimension underpinning successful economic development; (2) the consequent advantages of applying cultural, including arts, activity in the service of development; and (3) the corresponding desirability of introducing arts programmes that take account of cultural and social needs (Butchard, 1995: 7).[29]

According to the concluding paragraph (2.6.1) in the British Council report (Butchard, 1995: 19) the following main components of 'culture and development' exist:

1 A holistic approach to development, taking account of the cultures of target populations.

2 The centrality of cultural identity as a basis for national unity and sustainable development.

3 The inseparability of cultural identity and the preservation of the cultural heritage.

4 The inseparability of cultural identity and cultural diversity, and the need to preserve the latter as an instrument of conflict resolution.

5   The inseparability of the principles of cultural diversity and of universal human rights.

6   The inseparability of the cultural and the natural heritage.

A more recent donor document on 'culture and development' was published in 2000 by the Department for International Development Cooperation (Ministry of Foreign Affairs) of Finland: 'Navigating Culture: a Road Map to Culture and Development' (Seppälä and Vairio-Mattila, 2000). The booklet is not meant to be a policy paper as such, but rather a practical manual in the field of 'culture and development' for employees of donor organisations and development practitioners, offering practical approaches to integrating cultural dimensions in programme implementation.

HIVOS, a Dutch multilateral funding agency (NGO), produced the most recent 'arts and culture' policy document discussed here. Founded in 1995, HIVOS has from the start held the view (2002: 10) that while recognising the critical, thought-provoking role of the arts, it should not regard art and culture[30] as 'instruments' or as a convenient package for the communication of certain messages, as is often the case in the development sector.[31] This standpoint implies that the programme emphasises artistic activities rather than cultural ones. HIVOS considers arts and culture to be instrumental in achieving diversity and pluralism. Artists often have the capacity and social leverage to provoke, through their art, a debate on issues too contentious to address in public because of political, cultural or religious content. Artists can question issues in a creative, eye-opening and sometimes confrontational way.

The World Bank developed an interest in the topic, too, but from a different perspective and with a different focus. During the early 1990s the World Bank's former vice-president Ismail Serageldin (1991:10) made a strong plea for the 'cultural sector' to be taken seriously as a contribution to economic development. The World Bank had initiated a lending programme for culture and development by hosting its first international conference 'Culture and Development at the Millennium: the Challenge and the Response'. Held (with UNESCO's co-sponsorship) in Washington DC on the eve of its Annual Meeting (September 1998), the conference expressed the World Bank's recognition that the culture and identity of peoples is an important part of any viable approach to people-centred development. In this spirit the Bank has prepared for several years a new 'Culture in Sustainable Development' strategy. Moreover, a 'Culture and Development Action Network' has been set up to link the efforts of many organisations – public and private, international and regional – active in cultural conservation efforts.[32]

One of the outcomes of this meeting was that the Bank would only deal with culture – because of its close link to cultural heritage – as part of 'environmental issues'. It introduced the 'environmentally sustainable development' concept, embracing the cultural with the natural environment, and focusing on exploiting human and natural resources without destroying their environmental context.

The World Bank's interest in 'culture in sustainable development' deals with

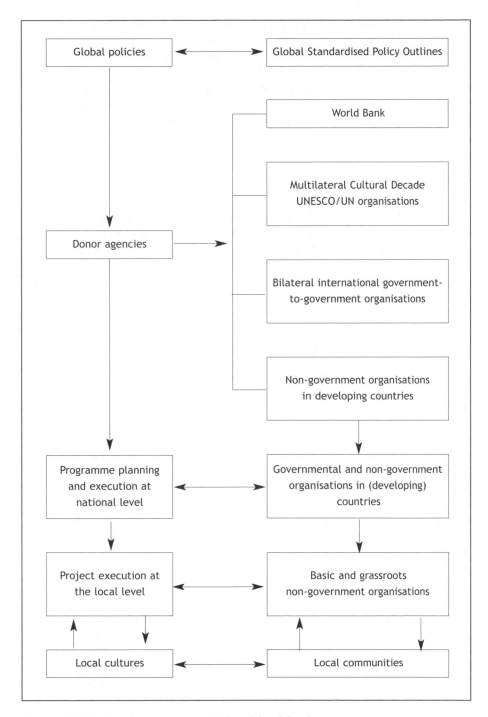

Figure 2.2 Cultural projects at global and local level

the intrinsic value of the historic cultural heritage of the past and the expression of the local culture of today, including the cultural heritage of indigenous people. These resources provide the benefits from sustainable tourism, without denaturing the cultural assets that motivate that tourism in the first place. Cultural tourism is considered to be a 'bankable' activity. Therefore, the Bank is in favour of programmatic people-centred support in the form of financing operations such as loans and credits. These new impulses encourage cultural diversity, support the maintenance of tangible and intangible culture, stimulate local cultural practices including performing arts, and restore heritage sites (for example, the ancient walled city of Lahore).

Cultural development policies

According to Watanabe (1996) cultural policies involve a broad area of activities: arts and entertainment, media, communications, humanities, aspects of education, cultural industry, intellectual property, town planning, the improvement of the quality of life, and the preservation of heritage (including the natural environment and tourism). All these activities are carried out by a variety of institutions, and cultural policy must consider all these in order to grasp the dimensions of public interest in the field of culture.[33] There is, however, no uniform way of thinking about 'cultural policies', as the root conception of culture – whether wide or narrow – will itself shape cultural policy (Matarasso and Landry, 1999: 12). 'What culture means for policy purposes differs from country to country. The Japanese cultural policy includes such areas as creative activities and cultural preservation, copyright, national language, religion, and the general way of life. On the other hand, the cultural policy of the USA seems to be narrowly construed in order to cover arts-related programmes, and thus almost equating arts policy with cultural policy' (Watanabe, 1996:147).

Although all nations form part of one or more supranational entities, individual national governments are responsible for developing and implementing cultural policies. 'Cultural development' is all about the development of cultural capacity (cultural infrastructure, institutions and policy, tourism, heritage, etcetera), which promotes culture or cultural education and hardly has a significant impact on processes of sustainable development at a local level. Despite this, most countries concentrate their cultural policies on cultural heritage, national archives and the arts.

In many countries the ministries and departments responsible for cultural affairs mainly devote their attention to the cultural heritage and the subsidised arts sector. Their policies often focus on the visual and performing arts, literature, festivals and similar areas. Under these circumstances ministries of culture tend to focus on infrastructure, especially playhouses, concert halls, galleries, museums, historic buildings and so on, and on well-known artists and art companies.

In looking into these plans it is striking that very few governments have developed policies with regard to the cultural industries. According to Isar (2000), the policies of individual nations hardly address production and consumption of cultural expressions as a major economic sector in its own right. Popular culture

– architecture, the design professions and the like – is excluded from consideration regarding these plans (Klamer, 1996: 19).

An explanation for this may lie in the fact that governments are not in a position to take such a proactive stance in designing cultural sector plans unless they create the necessary bureaucratic networks matching the way culture works in society. This entails an explicit acknowledgement of the synergy between the arts and education, the arts and economic development and the arts and social welfare (Everitt, 1999: 43).

Mainstream cultural policies reinforce the monolithic notion of 'national culture', focusing on arts, heritage and historical archives.[34] They do not deal with the cultural diversity of the country, encouraging self-expression and exploration at community level. However, cultural policies may have an impact on development when they aim at wider sustainable development and are based on well-established needs articulated by local people and founded upon their own development priorities.

Art education in nations takes different forms depending on the objectives it serves. It focuses on aesthetic understanding and practice developed through the art forms of dance, drama, media, music and the visual arts, experienced singly or in combination. Although these five forms may be used in interrelated ways, each has its unique techniques and conventions.

Although the teaching of art is as old as art itself, art education came into being in the early 1800s. Instruction in the visual and performing arts was then only available at academies of art, and only for a talented élite pursuing careers as artists. Towards the end of the nineteenth-century, art education was introduced at secondary schools in Europe (Goblot, 1973: 434). Its foremost purpose was to educate middle-class children about the general cultural heritage, preparing some of them to enter arts or fine arts education at higher level.

Today, there is a strong lobby for art education in Europe, initiated and supported by the Council of Europe, but there is no agreement on a common policy, with each member state going its own way. In the Federal Republic of Germany, for example, many art education programmes exist side by side. In accordance with the constitution, the entire school system is controlled by the various states making up the federation. Education policy was decentralised when the Republic was founded in 1947. With the collapse of the Berlin Wall in 1989, there are now as many as 16 states taking political decisions concerning education (Jentzsch, 1996: 184). School programmes and, in particular, arts education programmes in Germany include the visual arts, music, dance, drama and media.

In Africa, shortly after independence during the 1960s the young developing countries did not have educational systems of their own. In building them they copied the educational systems of their former European colonisers. The higher educational system in French-speaking Africa resembles that of its former coloniser. The English-speaking developing countries adapted the British system. During the 1970s people in Africa gradually began to ask what the place of music, dance and drama within regular school curricula should be. Through the years

Box 2.1 Cultural policy development in a transitional country: Romania in the period 1989–2001

There was no Ministry of Culture in communist Romania, but a half-state, half-Party authority: 'the Council of Socialist Culture and Education'. A Ministry of Culture was one of the first to be created after the collapse of the Ceausescu regime in December 1989. It had to deal with the question: should Romania adopt the model of a decentralised system of cultural institutions and reform their financing by introducing subsidies for projects and programmes, or should a centralised decision-making system with continued payments be maintained, irrespective of the results?

The first two years (1990–1) of democracy in Romania were marked by attempts to define norms in culture as people and institutions adapted to the lifting of censorship. Few intellectuals had ever thought about the reconciliation period. Soon after 1989 more than 150 political parties were established in Romania, illustrating the low level of organisation and cohesion of the country at that time. In the period (1989–2001) of democratic life, Romania went through four general elections, nine prime ministers, ten ministers of culture and a constantly changing leadership structure in the cinematography industry, the archives, the audio-visual council, the public radio, the public television, and other bodies. It is difficult to maintain continuity under these conditions.

Until 1994, nobody in Romania discussed 'cultural policies'. The former communist regime did not use this concept. They spoke only of 'socialist culture'. Many artists who opposed the communist official culture because of its foreign origin rejected postmodernist culture for the same reason.

An evaluation at the end of 1994 pointed out that Romania did not yet have a cultural policy. In 2000 a ten-year strategy was designed using the money provided by the European Commission in the framework of the Phare (enlargement) programme. This was the first coherent strategy for Romanian cultural development. At the end of 2000 a new government reorganised the ministries, creating the Ministry of Culture and Religious Affairs. A year later the new Ministry had no official strategy, although some non-official documents had been published by various public and private organisations in an attempt to provide direction to Romanian culture.

Yet, in spite of a dramatic fall in the state budget for culture (from 0.73 per cent of GDP, in 1998, to 0.078 per cent in 2001), a vivacious and diverse cultural life was emerging (Nitulescu, 2002: 6–8).

efforts have been made to contextualise African drama within the secondary school curriculum.[35]

At regional level, too, curricula have become more and more streamlined – in the South-East Asian region, for example, one of their official networks is the South-East Asian Ministers of Education Organisation (SEAMEO). As well as organising regional seminars, it promotes cooperative educational programmes. The SEAMEO Regional Centre for Archaeology and Fine Arts (SPAFA) stimulated the ministries of education (and culture) of the member states to develop a curriculum in the field of art education to be introduced within the context of basic education for children in the 4–14 age group. Thus the school becomes a main provider of knowledge of the fine arts and performing arts experienced by the child in his home community. In the near future these children will look at their local community life while applying national standards to appreciate local art. In that sense they will view the arts through the eyes of an outsider.

Since the early 1990s an effort has been made within the European Union to arrive at the 'internationalisation' of the educational system, including art education at tertiary level. It all started with funding programmes aimed at stimulating the mobility of students and lecturers, especially between Western and Eastern Europe. Later on, the curricula became more internationally oriented and were delivered in English. Since the Bologna Declaration (1999), moreover, higher educational institutes all over Europe have been working together in order to introduce the uniform EU bachelor–master (BaMa) structure, making student mobility within the EU much more comfortable.

At the same time, however, the funds enabling non-European residents to claim international student exchange experience have dried up, while fees to study at European higher educational institutes have been doubled or even tripled. Slowly the 'gates' to EU higher educational institutes are closing for students from developing countries.

Conclusion

Conventional and participatory development strategies complement each other: what is lacking in each is the other's strength. Depending on what needs to be achieved, the local context and the means available, a more conventional or participatory strategy will be opted for. By virtue of its goals and approach, TfD belongs to the category of participatory development strategies, usually small-scale and organised in the form of a project. Beneficiaries and participants are, in many instances, the same persons. TfD applies local knowledge and skills to analyse and solve problems. As an artistic instrument it refers to cultural expressions familiar to the participants. In the process of problem solving, TfD also makes use of and strengthens the cultural foundations of the participants.

In the present chapter a distinction has been presented between 'culture and development' and 'cultural development'. Although the international debate began with 'culture and development' during the 1980s, the concept of 'cultural development' gained importance during the 1990s, especially in Europe and specifically regarding the analysis of the transformation of East and Central Europe. The cultural sector plans of these regions, including the governments' most recent cultural policies, were designed to enable them to live up to the European Union's invitation to become associate member states and start accession negotiations.

The features summarised in Table 2.3 show that 'Culture and development' is not about culture *per se*, but about a practical creative action for sustainable development, such as poverty alleviation, health, human rights or environmental sustainability. 'Culture and development' is broadly speaking a framework (strategies and useful routes) in which cultural factors and actions influence the process of sustainable development at a local level. Creative work, research and education today play a key role in 'culture and development' activities, projects and programmes. Creative activity (including radio, television, film and video, music, drama, puppetry, dance, visual arts and crafts, writing and storytelling) already features in a variety of development programmes such as health and hazard awareness, human rights, the environment, governance, education and communication, skills training, structural development, conflict resolution and post-emergency reconstruction.

3
Using TfD as a Process and as a Product*

The above chapters have made it clear that the key words in describing and analysing TfD are: 'participatory development', 'participatory action', 'awareness raising' and 'culture and development'. TfD is about learning together through the arts, and about using the arts to inform and to teach. Through the application of local and traditional media and art forms, the cultural identities of societies are reinforced. In this way, socio-economic and cultural development go hand in hand.

Almost all TfD activities started from the context of non-formal education: a process of learning among targeted audiences, aimed at the improvement of sustainable problem-solving capacities in communities to enable them to alter their own living conditions in a more permanent way. Therefore, TfD is not seen as an activity on its own, but as embedded within the wider context of a series of other development activities and sectors (health, sanitation, agriculture) in order to improve the quality of life.

There are various forms of TfD. However, all these forms of theatre deal with national and local developmental issues, problems and situations. TfD as a generic term describes a range of theatrical practices and participatory methods to engage marginalised members of communities in a dialogical process aimed at enhancing awareness of political and social issues, building up social cohesion and stimulating the participation, awareness and organisational strength of groups and communities.

TfD aims at empowering members of the targeted community to become proactive agents in their own development. This is mainly done in two ways. First,

---

* Essays in Part II which relate to the contents of this chapter are:
  Chapter 8 Assessing the results of development activities
  Chapter 9 TfD and Development Support Communication
  Chapter 10 Forms and levels of education
  Chapter 12 Conflicts and the arts

collaboration in TfD workshops, as a learning and discovery process made up of a sequence of social practices seen as interconnected, is meant to create a critical consciousness and raise the awareness of the participants, enabling them to take action in order to solve their development problems. In this sense, TfD is always 'work in progress'. Second, change can be achieved by performances providing the community with information and instruction on behavioural changes likely to improve living conditions considerably in a sustainable way. It should also be emphasised that a *combination* of workshops and performances has been used.

In TfD, both theatre and development practitioners wish to bring their audience, target group or stakeholders to accept a particular line of thought leading to sustainable behavioural change.

Ultimately, TfD is a social intervention in which the process of creating a play is educationally speaking as valuable as the end product: the performance.

In the following paragraphs the process and product approaches in using TfD are discussed in greater detail.

Table 3.1 TfD used as a process and as a product

	Workshop	**Performance**
TfD as a process (people-centred and learner-oriented)	Individual changes at community level. Workshop (as didactic format) used for problem-solving purposes at community level	The working process of creating a TfD play aimed at creating social cohesion at community level Forum Theatre Community Theatre
TfD as a product (message-centred and sender-oriented)		TfD performance as a means to an end: focused on behavioural change in primary stakeholders by means of persuasive communication Entertainment-education: propaganda plays for developmental or political messages and advocacy

TfD as a process

The TfD process is a well-known practice at community level for analysing local problems. It contributes in a creative way towards local awareness raising and problem solving by exploring various solutions and courses of action. TfD is a research as well as a training instrument, and is all about discovery, learning and empowerment.

The TfD process links up with the human desire to answer a question, solve a problem or improve something. This is the most common way in which people learn. People learn by building on what they already know or believe. One already has a variety of past experiences shaped by language, culture, values and previous learning experiences. Learning occurs when students are challenged to go beyond what they already know, understand or can do, in order to build new knowledge, understanding and skills. Teachers challenge pupils by providing learning activities and experiences encouraging them to question their existing ideas or conceptual frameworks. These stimulate thought, inquiry and action. Learning involves connecting various areas of knowledge and experience.

Box 3.1 The educational landscape

Within the educational landscape a distinction is made between formal, non-formal and informal education. All three forms of education form part of and contribute to a permanent process of continuing education or life-long learning, and therefore are considered as mutually supportive rather than competitive.[36]

Formal education is the hierarchical, structured, organised system, from primary schooling upwards. It refers to a process of organised learning within the formal school system in line with policy outlines as stipulated by the state and implemented by the national government or by private organisations answerable to the same main policy requirements as stipulated for public schools. Non-formal education refers to any educational activity organised outside the established formal systems, geared to the specific interests and capacities of relatively small numbers of learners. It generally consists of short vocational courses intended to help them improve their living standards and quality of life.

Informal education can be defined as what individuals learn from each other casually and socially, mainly in workplaces, interest groups, community organisations, the media or in a domestic situation from parents, siblings, other relatives and neighbours. Knowledge, skills, ideas and attitudes are transmitted from one generation to the next through upbringing. Most informal education is not pre-programmed. In Chapter 10, the educational landscape is further described.

Effective education and training enable students to connect ideas, people and objects, and to link local, national and global events and phenomena. In this way students see various forms of knowledge as being related and forming parts of a larger whole.

TfD applies didactic approaches also commonly used in non-formal and adult education, especially when it serves as a process at community level in order to analyse local problems. In the context of the Hamburg Declaration,[37] adult education denotes the entire body of ongoing learning processes, formal or otherwise, whereby people regarded as adults by their society develop their abilities, enrich their knowledge, and improve their technical or professional qualifications or turn them in a new direction to meet their own needs and those of their society. Adult education/training is the most important instrument or cornerstone in non-formal education for providing adults with tools to change their socio-economic position by teaching them new skills.

During the last decade or so, training has become a common activity in all development projects. Training is understood to be a structured, deliberate, directed and purposive learning intervention. However, when related to social development training does not focus on information giving or skill building but encourages its practitioners to articulate their own knowledge and needs, to know and learn more. This principle is the same for any programme, whether dealing with sanitation, forestry, health, childcare, income-generating activities, food preservation or credit and savings.

In participatory training learning is a social event. This training aims at facilitating critical thinking. The group is the basic unit in this process of experiential learning and action. Preferably the training design itself is participatory. The following key features of this kind of training can be distinguished:

1 A central focus on the learning needs expressed by the participants.

2 A curriculum including access to knowledge, skills and awareness.

3 Experiential learning, as derived from the experiences of the participants.

4 An enabling 'learning environment', providing security within which to share and experiment with the 'lessons learned'.

5 The trainer is a facilitator more than a teacher.

6 Alongside the development of 'critical thinking', the useful knowledge of the dominant mainstream system is explained.

Participatory training is meant to enable trainees to gain control over their lives in a more active manner, to facilitate the breaking of the 'culture of silence', to instill confidence, to express the individual and the collective interest, and to aid understanding of social dynamics and the identification of solutions.[38]

The following paragraphs discuss the workshop as the most common format for participatory learning activities, and participatory research as an important instrument in identifying and analysing common problems.

Workshops

The term 'workshop' refers to a well-planned but sufficiently flexible process in which the members of a target group meet and are provided with a frame of reference. Here the learning process aims to enable the individual participants to interpret and handle their own experiences in a more efficient, effective and adequate way than before.

Although an important component of workshops is to share information, participate in discussion and experiment with future action strategies, workshops are practical in nature. Their topics are closely linked to issues considered relevant to the group involved.

Workshops provide more than just learning sessions. They aim at an interactive approach to education in which teaching and learning are considered as partner processes. Workshops enable people to work together on a common concern in a structured but informal and participatory setting. The meetings provide welcome opportunities for the participants to meet others who have confronted similar problems and to discuss how they have been solved. People from disparate backgrounds or levels of experience are brought together. Workshops offer an exciting and creative way for adults to learn from each other, and to develop new ideas. Because the experiences and stories of participants are taken seriously they stimulate cultural understanding at a practical level and enable a deeper level of social analysis. This is why workshops are often used for training or for 'brainstorming' on a given topic (Eade, 1997: 152).

The workshop context must therefore provide a supportive, safe, learning environment in which participants feel confident about sharing and analysing experiences. Under such conditions risk taking is encouraged, errors are regarded as necessary and acceptable, and effective participation can occur.

Within the workshop context, TfD techniques (firmly based on local culture and traditions) may function as instruments to act out local problems or may provide a laboratory situation offering opportunities to *explore* problem solving strategies by acting out problem areas and applying simulation games to find ways out. A way to achieve this is by projecting issues and problems experienced in *real life situations* into dramatic scenarios. The audience is encouraged to be active and selective, to consider messages carefully and to experiment with alternative actions and potentialities.

During all stages of the workshop a variety of (drama) games and exercises are used, either as ice-breaking games,[39] or as tools for debate, problem identification and analysis. Introductory ice-breaking games (involving popular songs, storytelling, jokes, riddling, and other activities), are followed by short rehearsal scenes, forming part of the awareness-raising exercises.

Participatory research

Within participatory approaches towards development a bottom-up approach to planning and implementation of development activities is crucial. Participatory action research is used to empower individuals to take practical action as individuals or as a group, sometimes in cooperation with 'outsiders' often referred to as facilitators, conveners, catalysts, monitors or promoters. As soon as action research becomes participatory in nature, the researcher's position should become equal to that of the other participants. Instead of the individual researcher's exercise, it becomes the collective inquiry, analysis and interpretation of social phenomena within the community. Ultimately, it aims at problem solving and the improvement of the quality of life of the primary stakeholders.

One of the participatory research methods is called Participatory Rural Appraisal (PRA). According to Chambers (1994a: 953–4), PRA as it developed during the early to mid-1990s had various origins: activist participatory research, agro-ecosystem analysis, applied anthropology, field research on farming systems, and rapid rural appraisal (RRA). Under the denominator 'activist participatory research' Chambers refers to the Freirean approach to literacy as a root of PRA. 'Applied anthropology' (Chambers, 1994b: 1255) refers to the issues of emic-etic distinction and the validity of indigenous knowledge systems, integrated within PRA.

In recent years, the increasing use of PRA and related participatory approaches by NGOs, government and international agencies has opened up new possibilities. Now a policy can be influenced by those who are poor, vulnerable, marginalised and excluded from mainstream society. Practitioners of PRA have developed a wide range of techniques for structuring and focusing discussions. In one example, poor communities are encouraged to use common local materials (sticks, seeds, pebbles, stones, beans) in order to construct maps, calendars, matrices and diagrams that display their reality. This procedure helps them to analyse and systematise their knowledge, effectively communicating their needs to outside development workers, elaborating their own codes of representation, counting and comparing.

PRA activities such as mapping and diagramming take place in groups, working on paper or on the ground. The latter encourages more participatory behaviour, and helps empower the illiterate. Visual techniques provide scope for creativity and a frank exchange of views, while also allowing cross-checking. By using a combination of PRA methods a very detailed picture can be built up, expressing the complexity and diversity of local people's realities far better than conventional survey techniques such as questionnaires, which PRA therefore tries to avoid.

Most PRA methods and techniques are aimed at a greater exchange of knowledge through a dialogue between development practitioners and the local community. These methods and techniques are visually based, involving local people in creating visualisations and training them to listen to each other. According to Cornwall and Jewkes (1995): 'Visualisations provide opportunities for local people to explore, analyse and represent their perspectives in their own terms. People choose their own symbols from local materials to represent aspects of their lives in a shared medium which can be amended, discussed and analysed.'

Methods and techniques commonly used in PRA processes are:

1 Participatory analysis of secondary sources (the most common form is the analysis of aerial photographs, often best at 1:5000).

2 Participatory mapping and modelling, in which local people make maps based

on social or demographic, information such as health, available natural resources (such as soils, trees and forests, water resources), their farms (who lives where) or their community; and the location of other important local features and resources (schools and other public services).

3 Transect walks: walking with or by local people through an area, observing, asking, listening, discussing, identifying different zones, soils, land uses, vegetation, crops, livestock, local and introduced technologies.

4 Oral histories of crops, animals, trees and other resources; ethno-biographies of people, including stories, portraits and case studies.

5 Flow diagrams to indicate linkages, sequences, causes, effects, problems and solutions.

6 Seasonal calendars showing how seasons change and presenting complex interrelations between different factors such as the incidence and types of disease, patterns of rainfall, soil moisture, crops, agricultural labour, diet, availability and consumption of food, levels of migration, workloads, family health, prices, wages, expenditures, credit, debts and other factors varying during the year.

7 Time lines: chronologies of events, listing major remembered events in a village with approximate dates, with visualised biographies of episodes – diseases, for example – offering a striking way to represent historical information.

8 Trend and change analysis: well-being ranking, matrix scoring, impact diagramming, and innovations such as visual interactive questionnaires as an alternative to questionnaire surveys.

9 Daily time use analysis: indicating relative amounts of time, possibly related to the seasonal calendar.

10 Social linkage diagrams showing the relationships and local interpersonal networks within the community.

As TfD is participatory in nature and does not require participants to be literate, it is an excellent instrument for participatory action research. It can be utilised both as an element of Participatory Learning Activities (PLAs) and a strategy for implementing the results emerging from PLAs. TfD forms part of a visual process, as do all performing arts. The possibility of visualising conceptual steps in a process helps participants in analysing problems and solutions.

TfD workshops used as a learning process
Most programmes and projects applying TfD as an approach to facilitate awareness raising and learning use the following consecutive steps in the TfD workshop process: collection of data, action research, data analysis, problem identification, improvisations, problem analysis, script writing and rehearsals, performances and, finally, discussions and follow-up.

Collection of data: Information is gathered by means of conventional social scientific research techniques and/or participatory methods of data collection.

Action research: A multi-layered interactive shared social experience among the workshop participants which proceeds by establishing how participants experience, think of and conceptualise issues to collectively arrive at what they consider to be important.[40]

Data analysis: Analysis of not only the issues under discussion, but also issues of character and role, stimulating creativity and thereby enhancing self-empowering processes.

Problem identification: Initial formulation and identification (by smaller groups) of local social problem areas, perhaps resulting in drama improvisation and short sketches presented to each other, with the aim of establishing common action plans.

Improvisations:[41] Drama strategies favouring the use of more creative and explorative training instruments focused on 'discovery learning' such as role play, planned simulations and 'forum theatre' for dialogical group research. Role play and simulation games are often used as experiential devices to face problematic situations, to support problem analysis, and to come up with group solutions in the problem-solving process.

Problem analysis: Analysis and discussion are encouraged around the dilemmas and difficulties revealed in the dramatic action during the improvisations on the ideas and life experiences of the participants involved. By doing so, the analysis goes beyond the individual testimonies. In this way participatory research turns into participatory learning and vice versa. To offer maximum opportunities to all those taking part in the creative process, participants are divided into smaller groups for problem analysis, aiming to arrive at consensus on the script of a skit the group wishes to perform.

Script writing and rehearsals: In script writing, participants create and shape new dramatic texts based on improvised skits. They further improvise, act and interpret texts based on their own ideas and those of others. After rehearsal, the groups present their skits, one after another. A discussion of each skit follows.

Performances: In performance, one uses physical and interpretive skills, integrating the technical elements and conventions of drama in order to engage audiences in various kinds of communication; this provides participants with experience in communicating and represents their observations and explorations.

Post-performance discussions: The participants describe, analyse, interpret and evaluate their immediate observations in order to focus the discussion and to build consensus on different issues, while performers double up as interpreters of their own situations.

Follow-up: TfD workshops and performances require follow-up by means of (informal) post-performance discussions. Professional assistance is necessary for those participants interested in engaging in a future *action strategy* promoted by the play. If TfD is mainly used within a training context, follow-up on TfD workshops is just as important as the process of learning TfD skills.

The TfD research and learning methodology is based on collective work and active participation. Though the individual growth of each participant is the most essential outcome, the main purpose is to strengthen the collective. TfD skills are instrumental in empowering individuals, in giving them self-confidence and broadening their horizons. Through TfD they are liberated from reliance on what particular people, each with particular interests, tell them. They know what is going on and join discussions more confidently.

TfD makes people aware of power relationships within the community and society at large. In a practical sense this growing awareness may strengthen the development of local organisations, leadership and negotiating skills.

TfD as a product

Performances when used for promotional and educational purposes are message-rather than learning-oriented. The main objective of this use of theatre is to inform people of important developmental issues at national as well as local level, and to persuade them to change their behaviour. In this way TfD has regularly served as a means of political advocacy and mobilisation campaigns in support of national development. Common topics in these TfD performances are: population education, civics education, voter education, hygiene and the disposal of sewage, water and sanitation, women's rights and violence against women, child abuse and prostitution, sugar daddies, the problem of street children, literacy, environment, health education, HIV/AIDS.

Applying TfD to convey a message is evidently synonymous with, or a direct result of, the diffusion model of development communication in which members of the outside group act as experts bringing new ideas and development programmes to the oppressed (Okagbu, 1998: 32). In fact, the use of TfD to promote safe sex, the daily practice of tooth brushing, or the use of clean water does not substantially differ from promoting a new brand of hair dye, a new bleaching product, a new brand of detergent, a movie or a book, a specific political party or Coca-Cola. It is based on the same communicative and persuasive principles underpinning the rhetoric of any informational or advertising campaign.

When TfD products are used in live performances, however, they offer opportunities for discussion and learning. They act as teaching material to inform, to create awareness and to stimulate a discussion. In addition, they bring people together, offering opportunities for social interaction and decision making. As summarised by Mda (1993: 178–9), TfD performances enable two-way communication within the community; community discussion and decision making; intra-village solidarity; and inter-village solidarity.

1 *Two-way communication:* TfD performances enable the community to take collective action by beginning a public dialogue, a two-way communication process with inbuilt feedback within the community or even beyond. All stakeholders have the opportunity to express their views, and to engage with the perceptions and priorities of others.

Box 3.2 Drama and environmental education at primary schools (India)

In 1949 Mrinalini Sarabhai formed the dance group Darpana and a school to train classical dancers: the Darpana Academy of Performing Arts, based in Ahmedabad. The academy has become increasingly involved in setting up an arts-based continuing educational training programme. School teachers receive in-service training in how the arts can improve and widen their teaching skills. They are also trained in using the performing arts to increase awareness among their students on subjects such as ecology, history, religion and literature.

One bridge that the Darpana Academy has built between professional art education and basic education is its school project on environmental issues, Jagruti. This was realised in close cooperation with the Centre for Environmental Education (CEE), and involved researching and workshopping a number of different environmental issues. ETC India, a large entertainment and communications company based in New Delhi, funded this project. Initiated at four municipal and four private schools, it aimed at sensitising and initiating action amongst school children to care for and protect various resources in their natural environment. In the 1994–5 curriculum the three topics identified for the programme were water, garbage and energy.

The academy artists used drama, dance, songs and puppets to stage a performance on each issue at the schools participating in the project. Post-performance activities included sixth graders (aged 10–12). In each school two teachers were selected to take part in the project and receive in-service training, partly through the Centre for Environmental Education.

In order to make the topic of water educative and entertaining at the same time, performances depicted the social consequences of the perpetual shortage of water. Other themes presented during the play's performance were: pollution, industrial waste, disease and deforestation.

One of the post-performance activities undertaken in 1994 was a modest survey conducted by the children at their homes. They were asked to describe the various ways in which water was obtained (piping or carrying buckets to the house) and the ways it was used at home (cooking, washing, etcetera). In the classroom a drop of water was studied through a microscope. Other samples were taken from a nearby river and from a tap in order to compare the bacterial content.

Their next assignment was to check all the leaking taps at school. At first the pupils could not understand why nobody was able to stop the taps from leaking. When they asked their teachers, it was explained that the latter did not have the authority to get things fixed. The pupils then went to the principal who told them that it was the responsibility of the municipality to authorise repairs and maintenance within the schools. Finally, the children wrote a letter to these officials, which the teachers and the principal signed. In this way drama and action research were combined.[42]

2 *Discussion and decision making:* TfD performances (as codifications of reality) enable participants to indulge in group discussion, affording them the opportunity to examine issues critically and then decide and implement solutions to their localised problems.

3 *Intra-village solidarity:* TfD performances enable a more active participation in social and cultural activities within the community, fostering solidarity among community members. By attending performances they are drawn into the discussion of common problems, and learn to work out solutions as a community rather than as individuals. A growing social cohesion is created.

4 *Inter-village solidarity:* TfD performances attract members of neighbouring villages or communities to participate in sharing their experiences and problems. These connections make for inter-village solidarity.

That TfD works not only at community or village level, but at any level where a group of people shares a common problem is illustrated by the example of the use of drama at primary schools in India, presented in Box 3.2.

Around the world, TfD performances have served as components of national campaigns on various topics, such as the improvement of health conditions and the promotion of literacy. The success of performances in promotional activities can be explained by at least two factors: (1) performances are accessible media for all audiences for whom the oral tradition is still the most important channel of communication, and (2) performing arts enable a face-to-face interaction between actors and audience.

Performances are accessible and direct media

Why are performances popular and useful as learning instruments? The answer is that performances consist of scenes, sounds and sights which are familiar, immediate and often entertaining. In many societies the oral tradition is still strong at a community level and is closely associated with local ways of expressing. The power of the spoken word is strong in its performance(s), as well as in the way performances are kept alive in ongoing learning processes. Oral expression can exist and mainly has existed without any writing at all, whereas writing is always dependent on orality (Ong, 1993: 8).

Oral communication manifests itself in storytelling. Local communities possess a wealth of oral literature: life histories, testimonies and other stories.[43] Storytelling is not only entertaining, but also educative in nature. Stories transfer social and cultural knowledge, through episodes involving human as well as animal characters, in order to depict human weaknesses and foibles. The narrator's creativity is directly experienced by his audience. He uses symbolic, pictorial, humorous, 'imprecise' language to tell his stories, embedded in the melody, lyric, rhythm, motion, image, design and colour of a song, dance, legend, poem, theatre or script.

Most local community networks regularly organise recurrent feasts and festivals in which the cultural practices of a still living orality come into the open. Traditional media, performing arts and sports add a festive note to these occasions. Oral forms of expression form part of local performing arts by way of puppetry, clowning, storytelling, proverbs, riddles, plays and drama. Music and songs are usually incorporated. Oral media and performing arts have the power to make people curious.

The oral tradition's performative nature makes it ideally suited to transferring educational messages, either through face-to-face and voice-to-voice communication or via radio and cassettes.

It is true that most oral traditions within the various cultures and ethnic groups are gradually losing their traditional value. In a society in which formal education and modern mass media have been introduced the storytelling function is taken over by other media. One challenge faced by the performing arts is to maintain and adapt their educational function against this transitional background.

Performing arts are collective art forms as they involve a face-to-face interaction between an audience and the performers. They stir emotional, cognitive and physical responses by making the audience laugh or cry or feel other emotions through plays and performances. At community level, local performing arts, and theatre in particular, fulfil various functions within the community. Schechner (2002: 38) distinguishes several functions of performance: to entertain; to make something beautiful; to mark or change identity; to make or foster community; to heal; to teach, persuade, or convince; and to deal with the sacred. Another function should be added: to inform. Whatever the message may be, the performance must reach a certain quality in order to entertain the public. The performance's exploratory, educational and persuasive element will always depend for its effect on the standard of entertainment.

Performing arts never exist as an isolated phenomenon, but are fully integrated into the cultural life of the society in which they have developed. In a number of regions drama is an important part of religious life and belief systems; and in other areas it is included in the entertainment industry (the make-believe system). Local performing arts (for instance, narrative art, theatre, mask and puppet play, dance and music) consist of cultural products and practices designed and produced by the people themselves. These art forms are disseminated and consumed among broad layers of society, and through them people experience their culture, identity, self-image and values.

Local performing arts genres vary from region to region. In Asia, particularly, the local performing arts are still largely a living tradition. Performances of local genres (*tamasha* and *nautanki*) in Indian villages are usually informal (though often lengthy) open-air affairs. Personal or communal festivities provide the occasion for a folk media performance. The repertory of most local performing arts (such as puppetry) is still religious in nature.

Here we encounter a delicate issue: how to use local forms of performing arts for development purposes without corrupting the stylistic rules of the genre for the sake of results. Puppetry has always been a favoured instrument for conveying information. The same can be said of various song and dance styles. Puppetry, however, has a proven capability to motivate people or to inform them of governmental services. For analytical purposes, such as in the problem-solving process, more verbal theatrical formats have an advantage.

Box 3.3 Popular theatre in India

Local forms of performing arts can be regarded as the root of popular theatre in India. Religious and commercial forms of performing arts, including narrative ballads and puppetry, can be distinguished. They have a limited number of subjects – either religious, social or romantic – and have long been used as educational media. Social themes have been especially prominent through the ages, with protest songs and plays raising a voice against social oppression.

Street theatre is also quite popular in India. It was taken up by the Indian People's Theatre Association (IPTA), for political advocacy purposes during the 1940s. In rural areas, too, theatre was used as a tool for building social awareness. An example of this is the work done during the 1970s by the Action for Cultural and Political Change (ACPC) in order to mobilise and organise 'untouchables' in Tamil Nadu.

During the last two decades experiments have been undertaken to design new local performing arts and popular media genres of a more secular nature, and to use these in the context of participatory rural development, making people aware of problem areas and informing them of ways to take action. Adapted versions of local theatre forms have been used rashly in the framework of information campaigns about health care, hygiene, agriculture, birth control and political lobbying – not always with success, as not every local expressive medium serves to bring a particular message across.

Since the mid-1970s the use of theatre has been the responsibility primarily of the numerous Social Action Groups (SAGs): 'Given the Indians' inherent taste for theatre, it is hardly surprising that SAG workers should have seen its potential as a means for educating and conscientising the rural masses. Several SAGs operate more than one theatre group, and their daily performances in the villages are seen as a vital means of developing awareness of social and political issues among the poor' (Srampickal and Boon, 1998: 135)

TfD and health campaigns

Health is one of several sectors that have felt attracted to applying TfD as a development support device. Initially performing arts served to explain to targeted audiences at community level the bare essentials of all kinds of preventive health care for diseases such as malaria, scabies, diarrhoea and leprosy. Using theatre groups to spread health care messages was a booming business during the 1990s among local semi-professional performing artists, including actors, musicians and dancers. Then came health campaigns dealing with AIDS in order to make people aware of how to prevent HIV and other sexually transmitted diseases (STDs).

Stigma and discrimination have limited the success achieved during twenty years of prevention and struggle against HIV/AIDS which is spreading exponentially – especially in Africa, Asia and Eastern Europe – and causing the deaths of 3 million people a year.[44] Therefore, targeted audiences (sex workers, housewives, teenage girls, truck drivers) are approached by means of theatre performances and workshops that inform them of the technicalities of prevention and the consequences of the disease in the long run, not only for the individual but also for the family and the community at large.

In the course of these sessions questions are answered: AIDS cannot be spread by touching or holding hands, nor through food, water, toilets, bedding or mosquitos. In addition, messages are disseminated advising people to stick to one sexual partner; not to have sex with someone who has had sex with many others; to receive injections only in proper health centres; to ensure that instruments for circumcision and other rituals are sterilised in boiling water before being used on one person, and sterilised again before use on a second individual.

Campaigns like this rely on an ensemble of professionally trained actors. Besides their performances and their interaction with members of the audience during performances, follow-up actions are undertaken by the health organisations that commissioned the theatre groups to perform on their behalf. Facilitators provide practical workshops and training seminars while health workers and social workers provide further follow-up. Participants in workshops might be asked what they consider to be the causes of the disease: water, food, insects, poor hygiene, bacteria? Something invisible in the air?

Two acting styles can be distinguished during these performances. First, the characters on stage are realistic and recognisable to the targeted audience. They represent social characters from everyday life such as vendors, policemen, the girl next door, the drunken husband, the elders. This style is favoured when the story line deals with the social aspects of the health problems or disease within the community. In the second style, the characters are allegorical in nature. Such characters are used to represent abstract ideas such as 'symptoms', or microscopic entities such as bacteria. A third option is: to refer to characters common to local storytelling or performing arts traditions, such as the epics of South Asia.

TfD activities used within the context of health issues focus on immediate short-term relief by means of nationwide government-run campaigns, while in the long run the campaigns focus on preventing the reccurence of identified mistakes and health risks. In order to make prevention more sustainable in the long-term TfD is generally used and/or experimented with in workshops runs by non-governmental or community-based organisations at local community level.

Education is another sector which has used TfD regularly as an instrument in mass campaigns, especially to promote literacy. In Ghana, the TfD Unit of the Non-Formal Education Division (NFED) of the Minister of Education employed a theatre group consisting of twenty, very capable professional performers (musicians, dancers, actors). This group was Adehyeman, meaning 'Sovereign People'. The performances were presented with all the flair of a musical show or a concert party.

The TfD Unit played an important role in both the mobilisation and the recruitment of new learners, and in creating community awareness of the need to join the national literacy programme during the first half of the 1990s. It produced its

Box 3.4 AIDS prevention in Bangladesh

Theatre for Research Education and Empowerment (TREE) has developed a drama-based communication awareness programme on HIV/AIDS in Bangladesh where several important steps have been taken in order to develop health consciousness and sex health education.

The TREE Foundation uses theatre for research education and empowerment. Its philosophy is that being informed is not a goal but only the beginning of education, while education should be viewed as a process requiring mental and material empowerment.

This foundation applies this philosophy to HIV/AIDS awareness: 'Though the rate of contraction is still moderate in Bangladesh, the risk persists and is increasing, especially because of some fundamental social and cultural factors being prevalent among marginalised people: gender discrimination, illiteracy, lack of health education and consciousness, and social taboos that encourage concealing any or all sexual problems.'

TREE has developed a Composite Awareness Programme with sex workers, who consider themselves unchaste and excluded, have little health awareness, are financially unstable and have little sense of 'sisterhood'. TREE enables them to form theatre/cultural groups promoting discussion on safe sex and sexually transmitted diseases. These are accompanied by printed education materials and information on basic issues such as law, finance and health. Intermediate results show wider practice of safe sexual behaviour, greater consciousness of sexually transmitted diseases and sex workers being empowered to lead relatively dignified lives.

Traditional local theatre is used to inform and generate interest in knowing more about and what to do about AIDS, involving the audience in post-performance discussions and question-answer sessions. A concert of traditional music is the initial attraction to draw people together in public areas (markets, parks, train stations). The hour-long drama is followed by a discussion session prompted and facilitated by the performers.

plays mainly in areas where recruitment was difficult and the communities were reluctant to attend classes. The goal of performance was to reinforce the lessons pupils learned during classes and to improve the attitude of community members towards reading and writing.

Prior to launching the 1994 literacy campaigns, the TfD Unit mounted an awareness creation exercise over radio and television in order to reach potential learners. Jingles were produced in the various languages of Ghana for promotional purposes. Special television announcements went on daily for more than three weeks.[45]

Examples can be drawn from other parts of the world. Mass mobilisation of literacy workers in Vietnam (1950s) and Nicaragua (1970s) produced 'literate' adult populations in a remarkably short time. However, the circumstances under which these 'crusades' took place were exceptional, with volunteers used mainly as adult educators. Their training took no longer than five days. This mass campaign approach (also applied in Cuba, Jamaica and Mozambique) eventually enjoyed a high degree of success during the 1970s. It was characterised by an overwhelming involvement of the state to revolutionise the social and economic structure of society.

During the 1970s, most literacy campaigns in sub-Saharan Africa opted for literacy campaigns in the national language in an attempt to avoid ethnic problems. These campaigns carried a slogan on their banner: 'One language, one nation!' Making an individual literate involved a choice between the local or the national language, and this was perceived as a political choice involving ethnic power relations. Today, many governments choose to provide literacy classes in a number of local languages, to be succeeded by follow-up literacy classes in the national language.

Combining process and product

In many instances TfD is applied as a process as well as a product. In other words, performances resulting from TfD workshops are performed for a wider audience with the aim of confronting the audience with the outcome of the training and learning process – in the hope they will recognise the situation depicted and start reflecting upon how it affects their own lives. Performances used for development purposes may, however, have been created by outsiders and not as the result of a participatory creation process. Development workers or professional writers may have composed on a particular topic needing to be addressed in the project or campaign.

In countries such as Zimbabwe, the West Indies or the Philippines, where community theatre has been organised nationally in a network and an infra-structure for training, the difference in the use of theatre as a product (performance) or as process (workshop) is not emphasised. As the key figures of local groups are trained regularly in both the artistic and organisational aspects of the theatre, the majority of these groups can deal with workshops as well as with performances. They are able to use theatre for problem-solving purposes during workshops, a kind of tailor-made community development. The same groups, however, can also be used during promotional campaigns on public health, hygiene and other topics. Here the dissemination of information through performances takes the foreground.

Community theatre
Community theatre is a form of theatre that shares its function and approach with TfD as a research and learning process. It involves a community in all the

Box 3.5 Community theatre

During the late 1990s Eugene van Erven, a Dutch lecturer in theatre at Utrecht University and one of the foremost experts on Asian political theatre, realised a special project describing the development of several good practices in community theatre all over the world. In his vision community theatre is an important device for communities to share stories, participate in political dialogue, and break down the increasing exclusion of marginalised groups. Van Erven has put together a comparative study of the work and methodological traditions developed in community theatres in six different countries around the world. A video documentary was produced to accompany the book.

According to van Erven, community theatre yields grassroots performances in which the participating community residents themselves perform and have substantial input in the creative process. Its material and aesthetic forms always emerge directly (if not exclusively) from the community whose interests it tries to express. Community theatre is thus a potent art form allowing once silent (or silenced) groups of people to add their voices to increasingly diverse and intricately interrelated local, regional, national and international cultures.[46] Yet, along with its participants, community theatre as an art form continues to be treated as peripheral. Community theatre performances are seldom reviewed by national media and, because they frequently occur outside 'legitimate' art milieus, they have tended to escape the attention of cultural theorists and theatre scholars.

processes of playmaking and presentation, perhaps leading to a performance in which the performers as well as the audience recognise themselves. Community theatre educates people through a process of participatory research and analysis, forcing them to grasp the underlying reasons for their material conditions. It forces them to utilise and develop their artistic skills and talents in an effective and entertaining way, to portray these conditions and the possible solutions to problems (Beukes, 1991b: 68).

There are countless examples of how community theatre has been used to strengthen cultural identity. Its popularity can be explained by the fact that in almost all communities the arts play an important role in the life of a community. While a number of works of art are presented in formal settings (such as galleries and theatres), the arts also permeate everyday life. Their influence is evident, for example, in the design of the clothes people wear, the buildings in which they live and work, and many of the objects they use every day. The arts are of importance to the expression of the life and culture of communities, contributing to the transmission of values and ideas from generation to generation. They play a major role in the forms of communication and entertainment experienced on a daily basis. In a world dominated by electronic media, community theatre has not only survived, but plays an important role in communicating for development.

Interesting examples of community theatre have been documented in a video documentary produced by Eugene van Erven. *Community Theatre: Global Perspectives* presents community theatre experiences in six countries around the world. For a full description of this video, see Appendix 1.

TfD in conflict mediation and the promotion of cultural identity

In many countries which had to recover from years of (civil) war and violent struggle, the arts have been used for purposes of reconciliation and rehabilitation. Here art is being used as an end in itself and the artistic production, whether it be a piece of music, a performance, a mural or a sculpture, is meant to contribute symbolically to processes of reconciliation and rehabilitation. In this way, works of art can bring together a culturally disparate audience, providing them with a means of celebrating their achievements in creating a new society.

When art serves as means to an end, it is the process of making art rather than the final result or end product which is important. In this case 'making art' is used as an educational or *therapeutic* instrument. Dramatic techniques are, for example, frequently applied as supportive tools in assisting traumatised children in former war zones. Visual arts, such as murals and textile weaving, are also known to be useful in this respect. Within training sessions the dramatic arts are frequently used for purposes of simulation and role playing. During such sessions one can prepare oneself for problem-solving situations. Within the regular system of basic education, 'arts education' is often combined with themes related to violence, peacekeeping, prejudices, ethnic stereotyping, ethnocentrism and tolerance. Within the context of adult education these dramatic techniques and games are often used in order to develop skills in conflict management, leadership training and community building.

When using TfD for mediation purposes, it is important to realise the potential of the arts to play a more active part in supporting the community to take control over its own development or prepare for good governance. Artists can act as mediators between the opposing sides, particularly when addressing the leaders of the conflict, and use their art as the vocalising point for ending the violence and seeking justice.

A striking example of applying theatre to reconciliation is the Palestinian theatre. This remarkable literary-cultural phenomenon developed during the 1970s as the professional Palestinian theatre in Jerusalem-Ramallah, under the varied influences of the Arabic heritage, old folklore and contemporary Arabic literature. This Palestinian theatre has also been inspired by Western culture and searches for a dialogue with the Israeli and Jewish theatre. Here again the intellectual heritage of Bertolt Brecht – especially his ideas on epic theatre – has maintained its influence. The direct influence of Hebrew theatre is also clear. Numerous Palestinian actors have been educated at Israeli-Hebrew theatre schools. Yet, while Western elements are incorporated, images from Palestinian local culture remain distinctive.

One of the best-known Palestinian theatre directors is George Ibrahim. He was one of the first to experiment with bringing the Palestinian cultural identity to life within this artistic discipline. Having started out with Jordanian theatre groups in 1964, he studied at the Hebrew University in 1970 and assembled his own company, directing Western literary plays. When not directing he began to write his own plays, mainly for children but including some for adults. He started the Al-Kasaba Theatre Company in Eastern Jerusalem and was one of three initiators of a unique theatre experiment.

Ibrahim, his Palestinian colleague Fouad Awad Nimer, and the Israeli director Eran Baniel decided to join forces in order to stage Shakespeare's *Romeo and Juliet*. These three very talented theatre directors, living and working in Palestine, transferred the feud between the two opposing families – the Montagues and the Capulets – into the situation in West Jerusalem.

Political and diplomatic uncertainties meant that it was not possible to start formalising the ideas into concrete plans until 1993.[47] The three initiators decided to make the venture a co-production between the Israeli Kan Theatre from West Jerusalem and the Palestinian Al-Kasaba Theatre from East Jerusalem. In their version the Montagues are represented by the Palestinians and the Capulets by the Israelis. The plot of the play has thus been adapted in a fascinating way to present a historical development in Middle East life.

Funding had to come from foreign donors. As the Lille Festival had chosen for its September 1994 event the 'New Middle East: Israel and Palestine' theme, it was able to guarantee financial support for this production. After this international presentation, it was performed in and around Jerusalem (Snir, 1996: 105; Delannoy 1995).

Further examples of applying arts in conflict mediation can be found in Chapter 12.

Conclusion

Impact is as yet difficult to measure: TfD does not focus on yielding concrete, measurable results in socio-economic terms. On the contrary, it is focused on results far less measurable in terms of strengthening values, beliefs and attitudes making up critical conditions of sustainable human development. Emphasis on outcomes should go beyond individual behaviour towards social norms, policies, culture and the supporting environment.

Looking back on TfD examples as communication devices supporting development, certain strengths and weaknesses are visible in its didactic and communicative approach. A SWOT[48] analysis of TfD practices would point out that its first strength is that it recognises the people's way of life as the starting point in development action. The second strength of TfD lies in using local forms of expression. A third lies in its being a process for creating critical consciousness and raising the awareness of a community, as a result of which they can then take action in order to solve their development problems.

Because it is so flexible, TfD provides many opportunities for independent and individual processes and ways of thinking. Therefore, TfD and other applied forms of drama serving as development-support devices cannot be entirely controlled. However, TfD planners and organisers are required to ensure that there are opportunities for TfD as a means of creative problem solving before becoming involved in any sector of development cooperation.

One may conclude from this SWOT analysis that TfD as a culture-based approach to community development requires an uncommon level of trust and respect for local communities on the part of governments, donor agencies and private development NGOs. Therefore, TfD modalities are not transferable from one country to another without an adaptation to the local situation. It cannot simply be plugged into a new context. TfD is a highly complex process and needs to be carefully tailored to each situation (Ross Kidd, 1992: 144).

Table 3.2 A SWOT analysis of TfD

Past	Strengths	Weaknesses
	TfD offers people an active part in their own development effort	TfD activities are too short in duration and do not provide enough exposure to new knowledge and skills training
	TfD recognises people's way of life as the starting point in development action	The economic return on the investments made in TfD is too modest
	TfD uses the participants' own forms of expression	TfD shows weaknesses in internal monitoring and inadequate attention to ownership and sustainability concerns
	TfD is a process for creating critical consciousness and raising a community's awareness, as a result of which one can then take action to solve development problems	Social life and (extra) income-generating activities keep workshop participants from developing regular TfD skills
	TfD supports participants in gaining courage to take action and experience the power to change	TfD lacks the power to implement sustainable follow-up activities, including personal communication, which is vital to its success
	TfD stimulates the empowerment of local communities and target audiences, strengthening planning and decision-making structures within the community	In TfD practice, it is often overlooked that promoting TfD in itself neither creates the necessary motivation for learning nor ensures the utility of TfD

TfD shows a strong potential to operate as a small-scale development support device in less structured environments	TfD requires a back-up by personal communication at local level through either facilitators, teachers or professional information officers
TfD is a culture-based, bottom-up approach to local development	TfD groups have their preferences when handling developmental issues. Theatre groups do not necessarily see promotion of human rights as their main aim. Their focus is on making theatre
TfD workshops at a community level are received by the participants with considerable enthusiasm	
TfD has a democratising effect in seeking to facilitate dialogue between the views and objectives of the elected government and those of the local community	

Future	Opportunities	Threats
	TfD enhances the awareness of political and social issues	TfD lacks the facilities of follow-up activities by means of training and logistics
	TfD offers opportunities to practise newly acquired development-related skills	TfD success on local levels depend upon positive relations between the community members and the authorities
	TfD enables people to take collective action by starting a public 'dialogue', a kind of two-way communication within the community or even beyond	TfD runs the risk that outsiders will set priorities and strategies, manage their implementation, broker all forms of aid, and perhaps even supervise the distribution of benefits
	TfD builts up the morale, participation, awareness, and organisational strength of groups, communities and organisations	
	TfD improves the quality of life	

4

Conditions for the Application of TfD*

At first glance TfD seemingly consists of playful, spontaneous and improvisational activities. However, the TfD workshop and the performance is a planned, structured and coordinated effort. Its success depends on many factors: political, religious and socio-cultural conditions as well as practical obstacles. Conditions for achieving the objectives must be favourable: room for genuine participation; sound basic conditions for local ownership; cultural openness to the approach; and the existence of opportunities to apply TfD.

The fact that TfD is a structured and coordinated effort may best be illustrated by looking at the TfD workshop and its performance as projects with a logical structure or framework. Such a framework[49] is a planning and monitoring device commonly employed when designing projects and monitoring their progress. This framework is based on the idea that the events occurring in a development project or programme are causally linked. In other words, it is assumed that if the inputs are available and the conditions right, the activities will then take place. If this is indeed the case, the outputs will be produced, and so on until the actualisation of the programme objectives has been reached. The uncertainties of the process are explained by assumptions (or external factors) at each level (Seppälä and Vainio-Mattila, 2000: 40) referring to conditions which could affect the progress or success of the training. However, training managers do not have any direct control over price changes, unexpected rainfall, land reform policies or non-enforcement of supporting legislation. An assumption is a positive statement of a condition that must be met in order for training objectives to be achieved. A risk is a negative statement of what might prevent any objectives being achieved.

The paragraphs below discuss the conditions necessary for the effective use of TfD from a logical framework perspective. Critical conditions and inputs for TfD as a process and as a product are presented systematically. Moreover, attention is

---

* The essay in Part II which relates to the contents of this chapter is:
  Chapter 7 Development support modalities and planning processes

paid to the intricate relationship between empowerment and participatory processes, the important role which facilitators and socio-cultural constraints play when applying TfD.

TfD as a process: a strategy for action

Table 4.1 presents a logical framework for the TfD workshop approach. The example deals with a workshop aiming at behavioural changes among the participants concerning safe sex, in response to the rapid increase of sexually transmitted diseases within the community. It is assumed that as a result of participating in the workshop people become aware of the dangers of unsafe sex, reflect on their sexual behaviour, and change their attitudes towards the use of protective measures. The hope is that as a result of the workshop the participants will actually start practising safe sex.

The framework presents the necessary steps in order to achieve the stated objective in a logical and sequential order. The activities in the bottom row of the table (Level 1) lead to planned results at Level 2. These results may have an expected outcome (Level 3), and a positive impact as the highest aspiration (Level 4).

In our example, the participants have been brought together to analyse problems caused by unsafe sex. They exchange ideas and experiences on the subject. Maybe they interview each other or outsiders about the subject. By analysing the findings of the discussions and interviews they try to find the roots of the problem and then identify impediments hindering the road to solutions. Cultural traditions may be one of the causes of the fact that people do not practise safe sex. Religious beliefs and unfamiliarity with contraceptives may be important stumbling blocks. These preparatory activities take place at Level 1 of the activities.

By improvising scenes illustrating the causes and impediments, the participants relate problem analysis to everyday life, common dilemmas and challenges. The performance resulting from the improvisations forms a lively report on their research into the problem and their quest for solutions (Level 2).

By acting out the situation and the topic, the participants work collectively on a problem and realise its dimensions. The exercise will, no doubt, lead to a better understanding of the causes and possible remedies, and may even influence a change of attitude towards the issue of safe sex (Level 3).

Whether it will lead to a change in sexual practice (Level 4), depends on a number of external factors. These so-called assumptions need to be fulfilled, otherwise the impact to which the workshop aspires will not be achieved. Various assumptions play a role in the workshop at various levels and examples have been listed in the right-hand column of the logical framework: Assumptions (risks).

Before any workshop can commence a number of practical matters need to be organised: adequate facilities to conduct the workshop, permission if required from the relevant authorities, enlisting participants, raising funds, finding a workshop facilitator, preparing a workshop methodology and so on. In addition, the timing should be right: a workshop at that particular moment should be appropriate and

Table 4.1 TfD as a process: the logic of the workshop approach

	Level	Intervention Logic	Objectively verifiable indicators	Sources of verification	Assumptions (risks)
Overall objective(s)	4	Impact: behavioural change	Condoms being used	Statistics Social surveys	
Project purpose	3	Outcome: participants have become aware and have changed attitude	Awareness raised. Attitudes changed	Questionnaires. Tests before, during and after	Availability of: condoms, funds health officers, adequate follow-up
Results	2	Performances	Performances have taken place	Reporting. Registration (video, photo)	Participants are open to the *idea* of change
Activities	1	Inputs: preparatory activities such as participatory research and improvisations	Preparatory activities have taken place. Costs	Problem-tree. Script. Other written or visual materials	Participants accept the working process
	0				Preconditions: adequate facilities (participants, facilitators, means, methodology, facilities) and favourable conditions

the targeted participants (the community) should be ready to tackle the problem and the workshop's topic.

The learning process should run smoothly during workshops. This cannot be achieved if the participants do not accept or cannot cope with the working process. Not everybody is naturally open to a participatory approach, confrontations and dialogue. Some people are shy, have difficulty expressing themselves, or do so indirectly; some are individualists; others are struggling with traumas or other problems. A workshop facilitator needs to possess great skills and knowledge of human behaviour and group dynamics in order to achieve participation by everyone, acceptance of the process, and agreement to work towards a common goal.

Another condition for a successful outcome of the workshop is that the participants must have open minds, be prepared to question conventions in their ways of thinking and doing, and be open to the idea of change. Those who fear change, or believe in the sanctity of traditions, may well understand the causes of problems but not be prepared to contemplate alternatives or seek solutions. However, as human beings are social animals, individuals can easily change their ideas in an effort to remain respected members of their group. Again, the facilitator will play an important role in trying to achieve an attitudinal change in the participants, a change shared by the group as a whole.

Finally, when people are ready for a change, the conditions should be right for effecting it. In our example, this means participants will need to have the correct information on practising safe sex, access to contraceptives, and resources to afford their use. Many development interventions fail because not enough thought has been given to follow-up activities. These should be included in the planning of an intervention right from the start. In the case of a TfD workshop this usually means ensuring that other organisations which can provide the necessary follow-up are involved right from the beginning of the process. Extension services, health workers, social workers, and schools can all provide people with practical assistance in changing their behaviour and solving their problems.

TfD as a product: a strategy for action

In Table 4.2, a similar logical framework structure is presented, this time for TfD as a product. The same example is used: safe sex promotion to prevent sexually transmitted diseases. Comparing the logical frameworks, it becomes evident that the overall objectives when using TfD as a product are broader and more far-reaching than those when using TfD as a process. When using TfD as a product, the aim is to realise behavioural change amongst those attending the performances, while in the TfD workshop the target of the behavioural change is the participants. When TfD is a product, the main activity consists of conducting the performance and stimulating a dialogue with and amongst the audience, whereas when TfD is a process the main activity consists of research and discussion among the workshop participants, leading to a performance.

In the examples of the TfD workshop and the TfD performance, the overall objectives are the same: to stimulate behavioural change. The scope of the impact, however, differs. While the workshop focuses on changes in the lives and social environment of its participants, performances are often used in campaigns with a broader national perspective: to contribute towards higher national objectives such as poverty reduction or the fight against endemic diseases.

In both approaches, it is assumed that discussions (between people) are instrumental in creating awareness of a subject, in exchanging opinions and in

Table 4.2 TfD as a product: the logic of the performance approach

	Level	Intervention logic	Objectively verifiable indicators	Sources of verification	Assumptions (risks)
Overall development objective(s)	*4*	Impact: behavioural change	Increased use of condoms	Statistics. Social surveys	
Project purpose	*3*	Outcome: attitudes of the audience have changed	Attitudinal changes	Tests before and after	Availability of: condoms, funds, health officers, adequate follow-up
Results	*2*	Audience is aware of the content of the performance, its dimensions and implications. People exchange arguments and express opinions on the matter	Awareness is raised. Opinions are clear	Questionnaires. Interviews	Members of the audience are open to the *idea* of change; they see advantages and benefits in the new idea
Activities	*1*	Inputs: performances. Discussions with the audience	Performances have taken place. Costs	Reporting. Registration (video, photo)	Performance conditions are favourable
	0				Preconditions: adequate facilities (actors, funds, play, transport) and favourable conditions

exploring courses of action – perhaps leading to changes for the better. In the workshop approach, these discussions take place among the participants, providing an input for their performance. In the performance approach it is expected that these discussions will be triggered by the performance. The discussion is to take place among the members of the audience, or inside the heads of the audience if they are not meeting each other in person but are listening to a radio play or watching a performance on television.

A discussion does not automatically occur. Professionals need to prepare and facilitate this process. Not a single TfD workshop or performance would lead to success and sustainable results, if it were not for the enthusiastic and professional inputs of the trainers and development workers. They facilitate the research and learning processes, teach participants new skills and allow them to discover their situation, their own strengths and their talents. Moreover, they provide the follow-up if the participants really wish to put changed attitudes into practice.

The importance of facilitators

The participants in a TfD workshop are the objects and subjects of the learning exercise. The process is learner-oriented. In TfD performances, audience members are the 'learners'. Initiating and managing these learning exercises is a responsible and sometimes difficult task. The approach needs to be flexible and the activities relevant to the local people in terms of improving their quality of life, strengthening the experience of a growing identity or the local organisational infrastructure.

The follow-up to TfD workshops and performances is just as important as the learning process itself. Many people who complete TfD workshops forget what they have learned simply because they require numerous interesting and useful issues in order to consolidate and further develop their skills. Follow-up meetings with their former facilitator will help them make the transition from TfD workshops to follow-up activities as part of everyday life. Audience members at TfD performances need to be stimulated and guided in order to take action on the basis of the outcomes of the discussions afterwards.

These planning, training, stimulating and guiding tasks are entrusted to TfD practitioners, extension workers and facilitators. They need to be skilled, knowledgeable, motivated and respected in the community in order to be successful.

During the 1970s and 1980s development practitioners were referred to as change agents. Those working in the field of 'culture and development' were called animators. Those providing information – using persuasive powers to put people on a certain track – were known as information officers; and those delivering practical skill training were teachers or adult educators.

Nowadays, all efforts in non-formal and adult education depend on the availability of qualified facilitators who are expected to strike the creative balance: on the one hand they challenge their audience without confronting them; on the other they remove the structural issues obstructing participation. Facilitators must demonstrate flexibility in adjusting their topics; much depends on their empathy for the needs of the participants and their understanding of all the factors in play. The facilitator must respect and engage with the knowledge, experience and skills of the participants.

Over the years, NGO development practitioners as external agents of change made an important shift in their approach. Previously the concept of participation related to the imperative for community members to take part in project implementation in order to acquire 'ownership' of the work. Now development by process requires the development practitioners themselves to strive towards participation in the lives of community members in order to have a shared understanding of community needs and priorities.

A number of facilitators are trained for their task. Others are volunteers drawn from the community or individuals living there for some time before conducting workshops.[50] Volunteers usually have a good standard of education, but may not have had any training or experience as facilitators. In the long run, the best qualified to carry out TfD workshops are those with special training in adult education.

It is obvious that facilitators have a strong influence on TfD workshops. In particular, facilitators need to be alerted to the importance of creating a positive attitude to TfD by associating it with 'discovery learning'. Otherwise, the added value of the analysis will be nullified and the facilitators will only be holding up a mirror, confronting the participants with what they already know.

Empowerment

TfD aims at presenting ideas and instruments that enable people to take more control over their own life worlds – in other words, to empower them. There are several definitions of 'empowerment'. It can be seen as a process that changes the distribution of power both in interpersonal relations and in institutions throughout society. Or it may be defined as the process whereby less powerful members of a society gain greater access and control over material and knowledge resources, challenge the ideologies that support discrimination and subordination, and transform the institutions and structures through which unequal access to resources is sustained and perpetuated.[51] Or, more simply, for primary stakeholders or immediate beneficiaries empowerment consists of gaining the strength, vision and confidence to work for positive changes in their lives, individually and together with others.

Ownership may be thought of as the feeling people have in making activities their own. If they feel committed to the objectives, and that they deserve the credit and the benefits, the undertaking is likely to succeed. (Seppälä and Vainio-Mattila, 2000: 38; Figueroa et al., 2002: 12). The degree to which participants identify with an undertaking, accepting it as their own, may be considered as an indication of the level of participation achieved. Ownership and participation are two concepts closely related to the process of empowerment.

Participation is a complicated concept. It has to do with future 'benefits' to be delivered to the participants. 'Participation is essentially a "learning by doing" exercise – plans are made, action is taken, results are studied, lessons learned and new plans and action take place. This step-by-step process is often referred to in the literature on participatory development as praxis, which means practice as distinguished from theory' (Burkey, 1993: 57).

Nelson and Wright (1995: 1) make a strong distinction between participation as both the *means* and the *ends* of development. In defining the end (where the community or group sets up a process to control its own development), it is thought that people should have the right to choose their own goals and their manner of achieving them. In defining the means (to accomplish the aims of a development intervention more effectively and efficiently) participation is seen as the way to define which issues are important and to decide how they should be addressed.

Yet, the notion of participation as the key to partnership has been criticised from both practical and theoretical angles. A major criticism of this notion is that although during the 1980s it acquired a firm, worldwide grip on mainstream development thinking, this endorsement neglected the fact that the concept of participation and the participatory procedures may be perceived as too complicated by local communities and learners. One of the reasons for this is that participation is related to cultural values such as social equality and democratic decision making – values not necessarily embedded in every society (many former Soviet states, for example). Participation, therefore, has to be learned and desired.

Development projects taken over by participatory processes often show the following cultural weaknesses in the way they assess or evaluate the participatory approach:

1 Local experts are often overvalued and often are not prepared to become involved with the problems of the rural population in hierarchical organised communities.

2 The role of women is often overtaxed: communities embedded within a society based on patriarchal hierarchy offer a limited and modest role for women in public life.

3 When dialogue is the preferred form of communication, the fact that direct questions and replies do not fit many oral traditions and local cultures is often underestimated. Such questions and answers are considered impolite ways of communicating.

The following lessons can be drawn from experiences of applying the participatory approach in development projects:

1 The fruits of the participatory approach grow slowly.

2 Participation cannot be dictated and directed from above; it is therefore not easily implemented in development projects springing from results-oriented thinking.

3 Models developed over decades in Western democratic societies will not easily be understood and adopted in the South.

4 Decades of development cooperation – following the recipe paradigm – have given rise to a 'recipient mentality': reliance on experts who are always standing by with support, advice and technical assistance.

5 Where survival is the first priority, immediate and pragmatic solutions are needed most; while long-terms solutions, applying participatory methods, will count as the second priority.

6 The core idea of the participatory approach is to focus on the daily lives of the people to be helped, instead of contributing to changing the social structure.

7 Due to didactics and instructional formulation, simple participatory methods may actually come across as highly complicated.

Sociocultural constraints

Many constraints prevent developments (prevent people from improving their lives). Constraints on the successful utilisation of TfD may occur at national as well as local levels. Several constraints can be distinguished, all of a sociocultural nature. Various cultural constraints concern optimum TfD results, not only obstructing the contents but also the working process. These are summed up and categorised in Table 4.3.

Attending TfD workshops or performances demands some time investment by participants. One is prepared to give up scarce 'spare time' only for a good reason. As TfD workshops are more or less tailor-made to fit local cultural circumstances in a very practical sense, a high degree of flexibility is required with regard to timing a workshop. In rural areas, for example, a facilitator has to be very sensitive about the place and time of the meetings, the walking distance to their locations, and about gender matters. The timing must be in tune with each target group's work schedule. If there is only one rainy season, people are compelled to maximise farming time, often returning home after dark, too exhausted to attend workshops. All this has to do with the local culture of work, social life and social relations. An outsider might easily disregard these delicate practices.

However, even where there is a struggle to survive, work is not allowed on one or two days a week (Christian Sundays or Muslim Fridays) which are often spent cleaning up communal areas or organising community events, and this socialising aspect can be combined with TfD activities.

The participation of learners and facilitators in the planning of location-specific seasonal calendars (especially the demand for farm labour) should be encouraged in order to minimise attendance gaps. At the peak of the dry (also known as 'lean' or 'hungry') season, many males migrate in search of temporary work, returning to their farms as soon as the rains resume. In a number of communities falls in attendance are sharpest during festive periods, when migrants return to their home villages for whole months at a stretch. Several communities also include numerous itinerant cash crop farmers who absent themselves for protracted periods during the yearly harvest, making a sharp dip in workshop attendance hardly surprising.

Other constraints have to do with bottlenecks, of either a religious or a political nature. Many authorities consider the reading of the Bible or Koran sound enough reason for people to spend time on building up a literacy tradition, preferably within a group context as members of a congregation. Yet, attending TfD activities may meet with disapproval.

Table 4.3 Constraints on TfD attendance

	National	**Local**
Political	Political instability at national level can distort the continuity of TfD programmes at local level. Changes of government can lead to the sudden discontinuation of all TfD.	By means of direct and personal relations within a community the local authorities can easily obstruct a workshop and its presentations. But, by the same token, as soon as local authorities favour TfD activities they will cooperate and stimulate the participation of their fellow community members.
Financial	Shortage of financial means will lead to a loss of quality in the entire TfD approach and might bring the project to a standstill well before it was supposed to end.	Scarce financial resources will influence the access of the co-ordinating organisation and the quality it can deliver; the training and rewards of the facilitators; the infrastructural provisions; and the dissemination of training materials.
Organisational	Keeping people ignorant, by obstructing attendance at TfD workshops, may well suit the mainstream authorities.	The cultural and socio-political gap between the outsiders (development practitioners/ facilitators) and the targeted audience.
Didactic	Theatrical medium may also be used by political forces and development agencies for their own purposes in terms of political lobbying and advocacy.	Workshops tend to remain at the consciousness-raising level.
Duration	Short-term one-time project intervention.	Limited amount of time available to the participants. TfD projects demand time investment from the targeted audience.
Restrictions	Repression of freedom of expression (censorship).	Cultural restrictions and local taboo subjects.

To local authorities displaying problems is one thing, follow-up action is another. The attitude of those in power, nationally and locally, can influence the development of TfD activities. That is why when organising a TfD workshop one should obtain the general support of the local leadership and community committees at the village level. Those in power will actively, easily and openly obstruct the raising of political issues that may distort (local) power relations – such as the encroachment on peasant lands by commercial farms, oppression by local chiefs, freedom of speech, land reforms, the consolidation of labour organisations and democracy.

Most TfD practitioners tread carefully along the thin line between criticising corruption or injustice and avoiding arrest, especially when actors have worked on a performance critical of local politicians. As long as it entertains, without raising questions about power and corruption too insistently, the authorities are quite happy to leave the drama to the actors. In communities where the code of conduct and other cultural practices do not allow for any open criticism, direct public feedback will be hard to obtain.

Another culture clash may arise when taboo subjects are at issue. West African health workers using TfD in order to address health practices around circumcision run into problems when referring to the genital mutilation of females: it is taboo and theatre is, indeed, a 'public domain'. More generally, in regions where for religious reasons the visualisation of living creatures is forbidden, communities will be less receptive to the utilisation of TfD. Large or small, complex or simple, these constraints determine the possibilities of TfD.

Conclusion

According to Nelson and Wright (1995: 8) power describes a relation between 'haves' and 'have-nots'. Therefore, in economic terms, power has to do with ownership. Some people are owners, others are not. The powerful perceive 'empowerment' as subversive – it starts from the recognition that people have the independent capacity to organise themselves and to decide on the appropriate methods and mode of development suited to their needs.

An important element in empowerment is the ability to solve problems and take decisions affecting one's life. Problem solving is often based on social analysis: finding the root causes of matters by moving from personal problems towards understanding the forces and contradictions in society causing, contributing to or perpetuating these problems. Most problem-solving and decision-making procedures are group activities, the result of group processes, affording people a chance to play an active and participatory role in their own environment.

In this chapter a number of factors influencing the successful application of TfD have been discussed. Political and religious conditions, sociocultural constraints and practical obstacles all play a role. The intricate relationship between participation and ownership is influenced by the social context and cultural values of the community where TfD is applied.

The majority of these factors lie beyond the control of TfD practitioners. Other factors, as discussed in the previous paragraphs, fall within the competency of these practitioners: (1) a careful planning and execution of TfD workshops and performances; (2) a proper handling of group dynamics and change processes; and (3) a provision of follow-up activities for participants and members of the audience to put changed attitudes into practice. It is a TfD practitioner's responsibility to afford these conditions. If other professionals are engaged to conduct the follow-up, the practitioner must provide careful management of the process as a whole.

The following lessons have been learned from the application of TfD.

1 *Training should be useful.* When putting into practice what they learn, participants experience, the usefulness of acquired skills and knowledge to their everyday lives. This motivates them to continue their activities.
2 *Link training strictly with current activities.* Participatory training/learning has to be practical, address immediate learning needs, and engage current (economic) activities already taking place within the community. In this way participants overcome problematic situations arising from the social environment and/or the production process.
3 *Understand that people have their own pedagogy.* Learners already possess their own pedagogy and learning strategies on which they depend in everyday life.
4 *Poverty creates its own conditions for survival.* In principle this means that all resources are mobilised and play a part, especially those thought to be lacking (like ingenuity and useful knowledge).
5 *Participation in projects is supplementary work.* It must be accepted that projects involving the local community rarely become the main issue in the participants' lives or a significant source of income. Projects are only perceived as complementary support to basic economic needs, and much time will also be spent on social activities essential to community life.
6 *Community participation is a must.* If one has the opportunity to participate in something in which one has belief and interest, new skills and knowledge follow in a steady stream; adults can be stimulated as well as educated to take part in the process of transforming social reality.
7 *The relationship between local CBOs or NGOs and learners should be good.* The relationship between the promoting institution/organisation and the community members is a basic component of participatory training and has to begin as an equal partnership.
8 *Follow-up needs to be provided.* This lesson is just as important as the learning process in ensuring a successful transition towards behavioural change.

5
Education and Training in TfD

In order to render TfD sustainable as a development support communication device there is a constant need for capacity building in this field and to train trainers, facilitators, animators and coaches. In the North as well as in the South there are only a few higher educational training institutes showing special commitment within their curricula towards Research and Development (R&D) in this field, and towards the use of performing arts in development support communication. The best examples to date are to be found in the North.

Several universities in developing countries have a national school of drama or offer lecture courses in drama and performance studies. Some also provide degrees in the field of cultural management, organisation and administration. In order to provide a fuller insight into their curricula, the contents of some specific course programmes in India and sub-Saharan Africa will be discussed in this chapter.

MA programmes and workshops

During the 1990s several higher educational institutes in the North started experimenting with Masters degrees that were very relevant to TfD. Programmes developed in the UK included:

1 The MA in Theatre and Media for Development at the School of Community and Performing Arts, King Alfred's University College, Winchester;

2 The MA in Multicultural Theatre Arts at the School of Media, Drama, Film, Journalism and Imaginative Writing, Liverpool John Moores University;

3 The MA (Applied Drama) at the School of Arts, Histories and Cultures, Manchester University;

4 The MA in Theatre and Development Studies at the School of English Studies: University of Leeds;

Box 5.1 MA in Theatre and Media for Development at King Alfred's University College, Winchester

The MA integrates community drama, theatre and video practices with development studies. It offers frameworks of communication through which specific groups and communities can further their self-development. The course provides an advanced practical and theoretical forum for students to debate how community drama and video can be made to work as a tool for development in specific contexts. It aims to promote understanding of the role theatre can play, not only in conveying development messages, but also in enabling communities to represent themselves. The practical and theoretical encounters of the course enable students to work with a people-centred, participatory theatre and video.[52]

One of the modules of the MA is an Integrated Workshop in Theatre and Media for Development (TMfD) (double module). This is a practically based workshop module developing the range of skills needed for the successful implementation of TMfD activities. It covers a range of participatory performance practices including improvisation, imaging, narrative, devising, group animation and workshop facilitation, and includes an examination of radical and normative pedagogies. In the later stages of the module students engage in a small-scale project in a local community, focusing particularly on aspects of participatory community research.

The Major Project provides an opportunity for students to run a project in the field (UK or overseas) which facilitates the self-development of a specific community.

Students go on to careers such as TMfD or community media/theatre consultants; trainer-trainers and TMfD project designers and managers; community development officers. They may also undertake research towards a further degree.

The programme is executed in collaboration with the cdcArts Research Centre within the Faculty of Arts at the University of Winchester. cdcArts promotes the self-development of marginalised groups through cultural engagement and the arts. This includes the facilitation of grassroots projects, the undertaking of training consultancies, the running of vocationally oriented academic programmes, the writing of print and electronic materials on Theatre for Development, and the fostering of networks for South–South and North–South dialogue and information exchange.[53]

cdcArts also runs undergraduate programmes which teach the theory and practice of cultural intervention through community drama and media (BA Drama, Community Theatre and Media) and of the production of programmes for the screen (BA Screen Production).

5 The MA in Theatre and the World in the Department of Theatre, Film and Television Studies, University of Wales, Aberystwyth;

6 The MA in Third World and Community-based Theatre at the School of Theatre Studies, University of Warwick.

The last-mentioned course has been discontinued, but the School of Theatre Studies at Warwick now offers an MA course and PhD programme in Creative and Media Enterprises and Cultural Policy Studies.

Not all of the above courses deal with TfD or community theatre as such. Only the King Alfred's University College offers a specialised TfD course. The other MA courses are more concerned with literary drama and its outreach to local communities. Short descriptions of the majority of these courses can be found in Appendix 3.

Each of these MA programmes offers excellent training resources underpinned by permanent staff with academic and extensive field experience of foreign drama and the practice of interactive theatre at home and abroad.

Within the context of course programmes in 'community theatre' or 'applied drama' the above-mentioned schools are keen to expand their research interests in

---

Box 5.2 ARTPAD, a resource for Theatre and Participatory Development

The Centre for Applied Theatre Research at the Department of Drama, University of Manchester, has been awarded a grant by the Department for International Development (DfID) for research into theatre and participatory development practice. The award, made from the DfID's Innovations Fund, will finance the production of a training/information resource in theatre-based participatory development techniques. Aimed at NGO staff with some or no experience of drama techniques, the resource will focus on issues of gender and social inclusion, new ways of participation and access to information and decision making.

The Centre initiated the ARTPAD Project (a resource for Theatre, Participation and Development) by starting a number of workshops and related research into Theatre and Development techniques in partnership with the Federal University of Paraiba, Brazil and NGOs in Brazil and Peru to develop a manual, video and training package. Thereafter the resource pack has been piloted and launched in Brazil, Peru (in both urban and rural areas) and the UK. All participants involved have been using theatre techniques in their work – some for the first time – and have given very positive feedback about the experience.

One of the most valued benefits of the project so far has been the opportunity to study group dynamics and the structure of workshops.

developing countries and community-based theatre. They appoint research fellows with experience and knowledge of worldwide developments in the social function of theatre and in its use in social and political contexts.

Thus a definite need is fulfilled for collaboration between Higher Educational Institutes (HEIs) in the North and the South, especially with reference to collaborative training and research in the field of capacity building and institutional development in 'culture and development'.

Research centres and institutes

At university level one is taught to reflect upon performing arts, while the Academies and Schools of Art instruct on how to perform in practice.[54] This distinction is very strong in the European context but certainly less emphasised in the US higher educational system, where theory (Arts) and practice (Fine Arts) are more easily combined – as the study programme and curriculum of the Drama and Theatre Department of Hawaii University (Manoa) and the East–West Centre, also in Hawaii, perfectly illustrate. Both training and research institutes focus on performing arts in the countries around the Pacific. As an institute dealing with intercultural and transcultural communication, the East–West Centre sees performing arts as a sideline. As a contrast, the Drama and Theatre Department of Hawaii University offers a unique Asian Theatre programme. In accordance with the US higher education model, it provides practical as well as theoretical theatre training. Moreover, research is fed back into the training programme.

Many universities in the North offer a special programme on performing arts in cultures beyond Euro-American societies. To mention just a few: the Universita degli Studi di Roma 'La Sapienza' (Rome),[55] the Catalonian Institute of Theatrical Research (Barcelona), Bayreuth University 'Schwerpunkt Afrikanologie' (Bayreuth, Germany),[56] the Department of Theatre of Wesleyan University (USA), the Department of Spanish Studies of the University of Perpignan (Perpignan, France) and the Department of Comparative Literature of Carleton University (Ottawa, Canada). Most programmes are specialised in a certain region. Rome and Wesleyan, for example, focus on Bali and Indonesia in general. Hawaii focuses on performing arts in the entire South-East Asian region. Perpignan, Berlin and Ottawa focus on theatre in Central America. However, none of the above universities offers a programme on theatre as a tool in development support communication.

The Theatre Department of the Faculty of Visual and Performing Arts of the University of Western Sydney (Nepean, Australia) works together with the School of Agriculture and Rural Development at the same University (Hawkesbury) in developing an intensive four-year study on drama and participative forms of theatre, such as forum theatre, as a means of emancipatory learning and action research in community development.

Performing arts education in the South

India

The National School of Drama (New Delhi) is the only one in India at the level of higher education. It is a state-funded institution providing full-time professional training for young actors and directors (Rea, 1979: 59). Students come from all over India as well as from neighbouring countries. After the first introductory year they choose to major in acting, directing or stage crafts. They are taught in classical and modern Indian drama as well as in Greek and modern Western drama. In their final (third) year they travel around the country by bus in order to study all sorts of local forms of drama. The school has its own company, the Performance Company of the National School of Drama, presenting a modern repertory.

Other Indian institutes work in the field of drama and education or support the research and development (R&D) of local forms of drama as well as contemporary and applied forms of drama: (1) The National Centre for Performing Arts in Bombay; (2) The Institute of Folk Arts, Puppetry and Folklore; (3) The Directorate of Cultural Affairs of Maharashtra State; and (4) The Drama Department of Marathwada University.

The National Centre for Performing Arts in Mumbai is concerned with the preservation and promotion of traditional Indian arts by means of: promoting stage performances in drama, dance, music and film; workshops, seminars and appreciation courses related to the above activities; archival recordings, both audio and video, in order to preserve traditional arts; and encouraging youth to take interest in the arts. The centre is not involved in any educational, social, or contemporary problems (such as AIDS), agriculture, the eradication of poverty, or the empowerment of women. It aims at promoting the excellence and creativity of art forms. If there is any development support message to it, it is incidental.[57]

The Institute of Folk Arts, Puppetry and Folklore enjoys an international reputation and stages performances all over the world. This institute has three core activities: preservation by means of a museum; capacity building by means of training; and performances. Drama teachers from abroad visit the institute to instruct, for instance, puppetry techniques. The museum is very popular: youth organisations, families and schools attend the daily performances. It is closely related to the Indian people's appreciation of puppetry, popular imagery and folklore.

The policy of the Directorate of Cultural Affairs of Maharashtra State is to preserve the cultural heritage of Maharashtra, to keep the people informed of its culture, to unite them on cultural grounds and to encourage the cultural institutes. A yearly programme explains the goal of the main project activities: direction and administration, including festival management; fine arts education (art training and research); promotion of art and culture (competitions, festivals, grants); financial assistance; and the establishment of Maharashtra Kala Academy.

It is an explicit aim of the Drama Department of Marathwada University

(Maharastha State) to focus its programmes, courses and extra-mural activities in order to advance the less-privileged people and groups in Indian society, and to explore conditions hampering them in achieving a better quality of life. Geographically speaking, priority is given to rural areas. The target population there includes those without access to basic education, numeracy and literacy, training in critical thinking and problem solving, and training in basic life skills.

The curriculum of Marathwada University's Drama Department stresses the importance of community theatre, TfD and training in other social drama games in the general process of rural development, including the use of existing folk media at local community level. The Department's major current activities and programmes, beyond the regular theatre training programme, involve the building up of research capacity in local media and performing arts by means of in-service drama teacher training, information services and skills training within a workshop context. As the sole drama school in Maarasthra State, the Department operates as an information centre, runs a modest library, produces plays and lends services to the surrounding communities as a resource centre.

This Department is opting for programmes which are essentially bottom-up strategies, capitalising on emerging self-reliance and self-confidence and preparing students for a more conscious attitude towards public services. It supports programmes which can effectively mobilise people into action, and which can result in social, psychological and economic benefits while stimulating initiatives in community life.

Against this background this Department feels the need for a more systematic exploration of possibilities and conditions for an effective utilisation of local media in development support communication within non-formal education pro-grammes. This not only calls for comprehensive research and analysis and subse-quently the testing of these media for their effectiveness; it also calls for the design and technical backstopping of a training programme in which especially drama teaching as an educative tool takes a key position.

Africa

At universities in Africa, the study of the performing arts is featured in programmes of various faculties and departments: African Languages, English, Fine Arts and Performing Arts, Music and even Adult Education or Extra-Mural studies.

During the 1970s, TfD projects evolved in southern and eastern Africa. These efforts spread and gradually took on a more distinctly African style, full of music, dance, and song, after the fashion of performances practised in villages for centuries. Nowadays, it is a lively dramatic genre promoted by university drama departments.

These departments have received support for such work from Western donor agencies as well as from their own governments. However, the attitude of African authorities towards TfD has been quite unpredictable: it has shifted from support to repression and back, since the authorities themselves are often the targets of criticism emerging from the theatrical productions.

UNIVERSITY OF DAR ES SALAAM (1980S)
The Department of Art, Music and Theatre of the University of Dar es Salaam has been actively involved in popular theatre and TfD in Tanzania, not only by promoting contemporary literary drama, but also by exploring indigenous drama genres. This Department has also conducted experiments, seeing to it that local communities participating in TfD workshops arrive at a process of critical analysis and local problem solving.[58]

The Department's main objective is to train and develop its students regarding skills in the arts, both professionally and academically. The curriculum, therefore, pays attention to the history of (East) African music, visual, plastic and performing arts. Next to investigating the artist's position and role in traditional society, studies have been initiated on theatre for children, creative dramatics, youth theatre, and theatre in primary and secondary education. Theatre and education at both the basic and secondary levels are covered, as well as the general area of theatre for children. The children's theatre project, as run by the Department, augments this: teachers from educational institutions are trained to work with children in the arts in general and in theatre, in particular. There is also an annual children's Theatre Festival.

The focus of research for both students and staff has been in the field of the traditional arts and their importance and role in modern times. Community-based theatre and theatre as an educational device in development support communication form a major part of the activities. The department trains students and non-students as facilitators. This is reflected through the productions and workshops its staff have conducted not only in Dar es Salaam but all over the country. Theatre as a mobilising tool has been applied in the field of health (mother/child care, hygiene, malaria, AIDS, drug abuse, etcetera), for the empowerment of women and in economic programmes. Although the Department's curriculum was reviewed during the early 1990s, these subjects continue to be part of its activities.

THEATRE AND EDUCATION IN NAMIBIA (1990S)
The two main educational institutions providing professional education in the arts in Namibia are the School of Arts at the Academy and the College of the Arts (the former Windhoek Conservatoire).

The School of the Arts is a faculty of the Academy (University of Namibia) and consists of the departments of Drama, Music and Visual Arts housed by the Centre of Visual and Performing Arts (CVPA). As early as 1982, the Drama Department at this School started working on Namibian themes and issues. It offers studies in drama, music and the visual arts arranged in degree and teaching diploma courses, conducts research and has wide-reaching contact with educational and cultural centres around the country. The Drama Department has its own modest playhouse at the University, called the Space Theatre.

The Drama Department aims to be instrumental in exploring and establishing a Namibian canon of dramatic art, a distinct process of Namibian scriptwriting, and the decoding and transcription of the Namibian oral tradition. In general, it works towards a synthesis of existing Namibian and Western code systems in order to establish a Namibian mode of expression. Its teaching and learning policy advocates a learning rather than a teaching approach; a process-based rather than a product-bound methodology; and a workshop rather than a formal class environment. Its work includes exhibitions and performances.

The College of the Arts provides training first and foremost in practical skills in music, ballet, drama and the visual arts. It strives for academic and professional merits in the arts field, endeavours to cultivate and equip future leaders in that field (through teaching, training and research programmes), and supports the building of a Namibian culture. It offers non-formal training as well as vocational training by way of specially designed programmes in all the arts. This training ultimately ends with licentiates or diplomas or degrees issued by external examination bodies. Providing musicians for the National Namibian Symphony Orchestra (NNSO) as well as trained music teachers for the school system, this college also contributes to capacity building by offering an in-service teacher training programme as part of the curriculum.

The position of the School of the Arts (University of Namibia) and the College of the Arts came under review during the 1990s in the light of the report published by the Commission on Higher Education in Namibia. It was considered necessary to promote research into Namibian arts and culture in order to inform the development of arts education, both at the future reformed University and the College. Therefore, access to and facilities for teacher certificates, diplomas and degrees including arts subjects needed to be improved. Support was required in order to develop curricula, methodology and the availability of a full range of courses in all art forms from beginner to degree level, with a view to finding a Namibian mode.

In order to provide the School of the Arts with a wider view on arts and art education, the following academic/professional activities have been pursued and promoted: (1) Decentralising arts education; (2) Furnishing new, and upgrading existing, arts educators; (3) Contextualising and updating all art syllabi on a continuous basis; and (4) Manifesting arts philosophies in practical terms.

The College of the Arts operates under the direct auspices of the Director of Arts Education and Training of the Ministry of Education and Culture. Of special importance to the project is the African Arts Studies section at the college, which includes Visual and African Performing Arts programmes (on- and off-campus), as well as developing teaching packages for schools in cross-curriculum and inter-cultural studies.

The College has a campus in Katatura, the Katatura Community Arts Centre, with the following course programmes: (1) a Visual Arts Department (offering a Degree Programme); (2) a Media Arts Technology Section (Offering a Trade Certificate Programme); and (3) a National Arts Extension Programme: Visual Arts, Dance Drama, etcetera.

The College of the Arts runs fifteen 'satellite centres' all over the country, one of which is the Katatura Community Arts Centre.

AHMADU BELLO IN NIGERIA

Art education in Nigeria is related to national policies and to the Nigerian art world. The National Policy on Education (1981) states that pre-primary education should inculcate the development of creative expressions, and that primary education should prepare the student for developing manipulative skills and craft training.

At primary school level Nigerian art education has been integrated with music and drama to form cultural and creative arts. The aim is to teach creativity, develop the child's basic skills in communication and to increase artistic appreciation of and sensitivity to Nigerian traditional music, art and drama.

At university level, at the Department of Fine Arts of Ahmadu Bello University (Northern Nigeria) one can obtain a degree in Fine Arts. This department also offers a strong community outreach programme, supporting several neighbourhoods to form culture-and-drama clubs as in other parts of Nigeria. Sometimes the performances are strictly meant to entertain. However, often playlets or skits are staged promoting better sanitation (club members have also organised neighbourhood clean-ups), AIDS prevention, the education of boys and girls, and peaceful relations between ethnic groups.

The Drama Department is often involved in producing. It employs club musicians and dancers to help train students. Community outreach is central to the Department's focus on TfD, to which all Ahmadu Bello drama students (belonging to an educated urban élite) are exposed. Pairs of second-year students are sent into the neighbourhood near the campus or to a village or urban area in order to bring about a performance in collaboration with local people. They discuss hygiene, child education and gender issues with people in shops and homes, and problems with local officials. Ideas are fed back, forming the resources for writing a play presenting the local language, culture and songs. Once the play has been performed before the community, the audience participates in discussion or debate dealing with issues such as AIDS and forced marriages.

Conclusion

The majority of the higher education institutes referred to in this chapter show a keen interest in theatre, including special programmes focused on theatre and education within the context of development support communication. Several theatre schools and drama departments have tried to contribute to training facilities by offering MA diploma courses for talented students. These departments are, generally speaking, looking for a direct linkage between research, development support communication and drama teaching – as the curricula at the Drama Department of Marathwada University (India) and the the drama departments of the African universities clearly show. The research aimed at here is practical in nature.

In addition, all these training institutes aim to initiate a supportive library, resource centre or data bank. They also share a cultural commitment to preserving traditions in the (visual and) performing arts. Some institutes even provide for modest museums. The final characteristic in common is their support of teacher training.

There is a definite shortage of resources and training opportunities for students with a non-Euro-American cultural background, and for students from other continents, to receive some part of their professional performing arts training in Europe or the USA. This situation needs to be improved. But it would be even more constructive to strengthen the Southern educational infrastructure by supporting research capacity in the South as well as institution building in performing arts education at the level of higher education. This could be achieved not only by way of financial support, but also by means of networking, long term cooperation and the exchange of students and lecturers.

6
Trends and Perspectives

'Culture is inseparable from identity: indeed, in many respects, culture might be defined as the outward expression of identity.' (Matarasso and Landry, 1999: 33)

This chapter summarises the previous chapters. Assessing the role TfD has played over the years in processes of socio-economic and cultural development, it discusses the strengths and weaknesses of TfD as an instrument in social change processes and the influence of local contexts on its utilisation. In addition, this chapter looks forward at opportunities and threats regarding the application of TfD in development projects and programmes, concluding with an agenda for further action.

Development

Although the main objectives of any form of development support by Northern partner institutions and donor agencies is long-term and structural poverty alleviation, the emphasis in development has moved from the economic to the social. During the early 1960s Western economists and political scientists began experimenting with 'development theories', drawing up 'modernisation' and 'economic growth' models. At large, national governments were viewed as prime movers in the process of development, while donor aid focused on supporting these governments.

This raised much criticism, and in response experiments commenced during the 1970s with the introduction of participatory approaches to development, mainly in the field of adult education. Local development practices focused on small-scale initiatives supporting members of local communities. From then on a distinction came to be made between conventional and participatory approaches towards development. While the approach to development expresses something about the way of working in the field, its support modality expresses something about the way development is organised.

International agencies have learned a number of lessons about factors increasing the chances of success of development projects and programmes. These factors can be summarised as follows:

1 Intersectoral cooperation: the most successful projects cross sectors, combining subjects such as health care, sanitation, mother and child care, education, literacy, nutrition, agriculture, reforestation and income-generating or income-saving skills with (TfD as a form of) development support communication.

2 Inter-agency cooperation: various agencies collaborating to stimulate NGOs to work with national and local government authorities (GOs) as well as with community-based organisations (CBOs) at a local level (and vice versa) in order to achieve more general development goals.

3 Follow-up: satisfaction through short-term results offers no guarantee in the long run that participants will retain their skills. Experience shows that progress is achieved over many decades rather than over a few years.

4 Long-term thinking: instead of many short-term, isolated projects, one might find in the course of the next decade that developing cooperation will be increasingly based on practical, future-oriented, long-term thinking.

Development cooperation could well be on the threshold of major reforms. Now, at the start of the twenty-first century a radical departure from the practice of the last forty years is under discussion. In the world of bilateral and multilateral projects those donating to development observe a shift in support modalities from projects towards programme and sector-wide budget support.

What might the implications of these changes in development cooperation be for the employment of communication media, including TfD, in the twenty-first century? The following scenarios are likely to unfold:

1 A growing role for NGOs in sector-wide programmes in which the implementation of an increasing number of projects is sourced out to NGOs, while the implementation of national long-term programmes will be decentralised to representatives of government agencies at district level.

2 Pilots in cultural innovation and training will be launched by means of projects. Project development is the domain in which non-governmental organisations (NGOs) have obtained a unique expertise.

3 Communications are poised to become a crucial area in development theories and the practice of development in the twenty-first century. The issue of cultural representation as a means of reporting underpins this new direction.

Development and culture

There is a growing consciousness of the fact that development cooperation, in addition to its economic aspects, also has cultural implications hitherto not granted due attention. From the mid-1980s up to the end of the last millennium, the world witnessed an increased recognition of the role of culture in development. At the heart of the shift were UNESCO's never-ending efforts, from the Ministers of Culture (MONDIACULT) meeting in Mexico in 1982 through the World Decade of Cultural Development (WDCD, 1988–97) and on to the delivery of the Creative Diversity Report in 1995.

The UN World Decade on Cultural Development was operationalised by UNESCO through advocacy using regional and international meetings, declarations and publications in order to disseminate the Decade's main objectives and its programmes. Major donor member states such as Canada, Scandinavia, the Netherlands and the UK initiated discussions at national level on the issue of 'culture and development', leading to policy documents that often included a section or paragraph on '(visual or performing) arts and culture'. That discussion on this stream of thought still continues proves the success of the first initiatives at the start of the 1980s.

It proved easier, however, to endorse the importance of the 'cultural dimension of development' at official level than actually to put the policy into practice. The reason for this was twofold. The winding down of the Cold War (1989–91) changed the foreign policies of the major donor countries overnight. It asked for a reallocation of funds available not only amongst developing nations but also amongst Central and Eastern European countries in transition.

Another reason was that policy makers persisted in thinking of culture as the 'cultural heritage' which should be preserved, or as entertainment at community level. They were not sensitive to its significance. In addition, it proved to be difficult to measure the impact of performances and creative workshops.

Despite these drawbacks the cultural dimension of development will continue to play a role in educational and developmental policies, practice and research. It is apparent that developing countries themselves are giving more and more weight to cultural aspects of development. This interest has become more visible in the policies of donor agencies, too. The World Bank's emerging interest in the economic aspects of the impact of culture on sustainable development and the contribution it may make to poverty alleviation is a very positive trend.

Power, politics and culture

At all levels of development cooperation a distinction can be made between those countries and/or organisations with the resources to think and speak of sustainable economic and social development, and even start field experiments in order to work and try out future strategies, and those without these resources. At first sight this seems to be a very outdated and superficial distinction between 'haves' and 'have-nots', between 'us' and 'them', between 'we' and the 'others'. However, it cuts deeper into the development agenda. First of all, it still is the main cause of many violent conflicts in the world. This is because, in terms of globalisation or neocolonialism, it touches directly upon ownership and property rights – financial, legal and intellectual – not only in terms of land legislation, access to natural resources and intellectual property rights, but also in terms of who is in the 'driver's seat' (even at a distance) of major global development processes.

With the exception of democratically induced government changes, all other political changes come by surprise. In the beginning this causes a period of political turmoil – for example, when moving from a one-party system to a multi-party system and organising general elections. In such cases, the first concern has to do with political reorganisation and keeping the nation from falling apart along religious and ethnic lines. This has its consequences, not only in the emancipation of cultural minorities but, most importantly, in speeding up processes of national development.

Growing fundamentalism will create direct or indirect restrictions with regard to freedom of expression, not only in Islamic countries, but in the West as well. War, military intervention and armed conflict cause enormous repercussions on the world economy and therefore on budgets available for development cooperation.

The cultural climate will change worldwide, too, whether we understand culture in its widest anthropological definition, or as the critical attitude of artists. Even before the massive attack on Iraq, a new McCarthyism seemed to bloom in the USA. Hollywood actors who publicly declared their anti-war attitude by protesting against the Bush government's military interventions in the Middle East risk redundancy. Not because Bush says so, but due to the Hollywood film industry's self-censorship.

TfD has been used for purposes of political advocacy by elected governments as well as opposition political parties. In the context of oppressive regimes TfD operated underground as part of the subversive activities of resistance movements. There has always been a fear within ruling parties that as soon as the majority of the rural poor start to break the 'culture of silence', this will bring complete destabilisation of the ruling regime. Motives to employ TfD in the context of these political changes most often had to do with 'identity', be it ethnic or social identity at community level, or the national identity.

TfD

Cultural practices, and the performing arts in particular, have been experimented with as support devices for development ever since 'development cooperation' became operational in the 1960s and 1970s. This first development interventions in which TfD played an important role were large-scale literacy campaigns combined with political advocacy and national identity building.

Besides large-scale national campaigns, one of the development paths which NGOs and CBOs explored thoroughly during the 1970s and 1980s was designing participatory approaches in adult education in developing countries using theatre and dramatic games as small-scale media to support communicative processes in non-formal education programmes. TfD practitioners and advocates applied the people's own forms of creative expression and local performance modes.

Which successful TfD programmes are still active today and for what reason? Are certain factors common to these programmes and lacking in failing ones? Successful TfD projects achieve their objectives by means of activities undertaken by local people after external support comes to an end. These activities have an impact on the lives of individual community members, the community as such and the wider societal context. This implies that the key components of successful TfD activities are similar to those of other development projects and programmes: sustainability of social change, empowerment, and ownership. At a local level, participation and ownership (the feeling people share in making a project their own) are stimulated in order to form a condition for support. It is considered important that the partner organisation(s) and the theatre groups involved view the 'project' as their own, rather than something done for an outside party (a donor or foreign NGO) or imposed on them by national authorities. Chances that the 'project' will become a success will increase considerably if participants are convinced it could help them achieve their goals.

TfD, in spite of all the problems, remains a creative, expressive medium and a powerful tool to effectively promote, educate and empower people towards a better understanding of the complexities of human behaviour. For example:

1 TfD gives a voice to the previously unheard members of the community.

2 TfD is pragmatic, somewhere between the normative and the alternative.

3 TfD confronts participants continuously with the possibility of making choices in order to solve their own problems.

4 TfD offers opportunities to *explore* social reality by means of improvising and performing for both utilitarian and creative purposes.

5 TfD offers a common playground or laboratory to explore near misses as well as golden opportunities for self-development.

6 TfD functions independently of the degree of illiteracy among the audience, because of its oral nature.

7 TfD uses the most important local resources: people, culture, tradition and language.

8 TfD proves to be an attractive medium because it combines education and entertainment.

9 TfD increases the participation of various sections of the community in social and cultural development.

10 TfD offers training in new skills and knowledge, encouraging participants to interact with each other and try out new behaviours; TfD enables one to take collective action by means of a two-way communication process, community discussions and decision making, solidarity and intra-village/inter-village solidarity.

11 TfD promotes behavioural changes by means of *persuasive communication*, stimulating changes in attitude, belief and behaviour towards development-related practices.

12 TfD motivates active participation in development programmes in order to improve the quality of life and in order to maintain development-related skills, linking them with daily practices.

13 TfD provides a context and the means whereby poor and marginalised communities may represent themselves, facing a wider audience.

Further action and recommendations

Experience with TfD over the last forty years has given us a fairly complete overview of conditions which play a role in the application of TfD and thus in the planning and implementation of TfD activities. On the basis of this knowledge it is possible to draw up a checklist of important issues to be taken into account when embarking on a development project involving TfD.

Such a checklist will include the following issues grouped into four categories:

Social embedding within the community:
- stimulation of a close cooperation with the other development actors (local government and educational services);
- support of local capacity building, leadership training and strategic planning;
- promotion of the participation of the local community and targeted groups.

Cultural embedding within the community:
- adapting the TfD activities to the daily life experience of the learners;
- support of the design and employment of learner-generated materials (LGM);
- improvement and support of access to education (flexible learning system);
- support participation of local artists.

Educational embedding within the community:
- promotion of linkages and interchange between formal and non-formal education;
- support of the design and testing of experimental and innovative curricula, training programmes and learning materials and strategies;
- support of the production and distribution of learning materials (training manual and additional materials to provide a methodology);
- support of the training of trainers, teachers and facilitators in TfD;
- support of experiments and pilot projects in TfD.

Sustainability of the development effort:
- to support the design of qualified review, monitoring and impact assessment systems;

- to increase of the effectiveness and efficiency of the projects by involving local research institutes;
- to support of umbrella organisations and networks;
- to support the exchange of experiences through meetings.

TfD activities likely to be successful are almost by definition *demand-driven* and *practical* ones. This is particularly the case in TfD workshops if they take into account already existing community proposals and initiatives and utilise an already existing community organisation. TfD workshops support activities carried out by the communities themselves in order to achieve very particular goals. This training complements local learning needs and the education is relevant to the community and the learners. Each skill the participants acquire is of immediate value in daily life. People feel at ease with the learning methods because they are familiar and functional.

The TfD case needs to be further strengthened by promoting interest in its application among stakeholding parties: governmental and non-governmental organisations, community-based organisations, the private sector, artists and researchers. They must realise that, if properly used, TfD is a cost-effective means of achieving sustainable local development, or of facilitating processes of national importance, such as the introduction of a multi-party democracy or the fight against contagious diseases.

Proper documentation of each successful TfD application and research into its efficiency, effectiveness and impact should form the basis of policies advocating and employing it for development purposes. Documentation and impact research should be incorporated within the research agendas of development researchers and donor agencies. The outcome should be widely shared with policy makers and practitioners. Moreover, innovations and experiments should be stimulated to explore, by means of pilots, the impact of new and innovative approaches in the social and cultural sectors. These pilot projects are necessary if new ideas about culture and development are ever to be tested in terms of feasibility.

The need for capable, well-trained facilitators, TfD practitioners and change agents has been mentioned above. Culture and development programmes are essential tools for a well-trained middle cadre in the field of sustainable cultural development. Preferably, facilitators should be trained in the country where they reside and work.

MA programmes promoting the practice and understanding of cultural action for change are in demand. Such a course should combine supervised practical projects, theoretical/historical study, a research assignment and a dissertation. The MA students receive training in workshop techniques, playing games, devising, directing and performing within the context of community theatre/TfD.

In Africa there is a shortage of staff trained in cultural administration. The training requirements of African cultural executives are immense, especially in a context in which the universities do not play a role. Such requirements are essentially of two types: methodology and access to cultural networks. Broadly speaking, *methodology* covers administration, management, implementation of cultural projects and definition of cultural policies, whether at a local or national level. *Access to networks* is fundamental, entailing a knowledge and understanding of both the cultural policies and the bodies existing in order to implement them (Roussel, 1995: 101).

Local governments, educational institutions, NGOs and donor agencies should be aware of the importance of creating and maintaining local education and training capacity for the application of the arts for development purposes. The higher education institutions dealt with in Chapter 5 may serve as examples. They offer special training programmes relevant to TfD and designed to build up capacity in developing countries. These institutes are also involved in academic research and studies that relate to TfD, (commissioned) policy-related programmes or technical assistance. The combination of teaching, academic research and contract research enables a fruitful exchange of insights between policy, science and practice.

Organisations including TfD in their programmes benefit from a well-trained middle cadre and facilitators. Experience has taught that organisations also benefit considerably from collaboration and networking. Concerted efforts through inter-agency cooperation usually have a greater impact than individual actions. Theatre groups especially benefit from networking with national and international counterpart organisations, not only in an artistic or methodological sense but also in strengthening their organisation.

Finally, governments and agencies need to recognise TfD as an effective development tool. According to Prentki: 'There is now an urgent need to root TfD firmly in the policies of aid agencies and governmental and non-governmental organisations in order that it is used constantly as part of existing programmes, rather than being either a light-hearted piece of window-dressing or confined to discrete projects which do not have an impact on the organisations' main work' (Prentki, 1998: 429). Advocacy and evidence of TfD's effectiveness will be needed if it is to claim the place in development policies that its still short but promising track record merits.

Part II
Essays on Development, Education and the Arts

Part II

7

Development Support Modalities and Planning Processes

What are the major modalities for implementing development activities?

Which planning and management processes are commonly used in conventional development projects and programmes?

Development support modalities

At present three major development support modalities operate next to each other: the project approach, the programme approach and the sector approach. Basically, these are different frameworks within which a planned series of development activities occur in order to achieve one or more aims.

The project approach

A project is a planned, short-term outside intervention in an autonomous process of change designed to achieve one or more specific aims. A project is nothing less than an organised, large-scale series of activities intensely focused on a set of objectives to be achieved within a predetermined period of time. The success of such activities depends upon several preconditions. They need an active support strategy (at a national level) and their subjects must be able to capture the attention of large numbers. There must be sufficient financial resources, a high degree of commitment by all involved and sufficient time spent on the preparatory tasks beforehand. Because they are short-term, projects are more open to experiment and improvisation than, for example, programmes. In terms of sustainability – measured by the likelihood that its results will continue to be used after it has come to an end – a project intervention must by definition be considered as a pilot, with the right to fail instead of succeed. The beneficiaries are seldom the 'owners' of projects, unless they have been actively involved in the planning, implementation and management of the intervention. Many projects are implemented 'for' the people by external organisations or agencies.

The programme approach

The concept of programme aid is built upon the idea of fostering recipient ownership. Fixed parameters and rigid structures are part and parcel of programmes, which, in the long run, are expected to cope with the need to accommodate complexities. A programme is a group of projects or related services designed to achieve certain generally complementary or interdependent operational objectives. Programmes are set up as long-term and systematic interventions and are evaluated in terms of 'sustainability'. The aim of socio-economic programmes is human resource development by means of 'institutional strengthening' and 'capacity building'. Generally speaking, governmental organisations run these programmes.

The Sector-Wide Approach (SWAp)

This approach to development goes back as far as the 1970s, but it enjoyed a renaissance in the mid-1990s. The sector-wide approach involves a meta-plan covering a country's development not only in managerial but also in financial terms. The planning involves governmental organisations at ministerial level, inter-ministerial coordination and a continuous dialogue with the bilateral and multilateral donor agencies. For most Northern European bilateral donor agencies and the World Bank SWAp concentrates on long-range budget support towards a select number of sectors in a select number of developing countries. In SWAps, ownership lies with governmental organisations in a particular sector. They make the plans, are responsible for implementing programmes and are accountable for the results. In SWAps the donor agencies try to coordinate their support through so-called 'basket funding', 'buying into' the same programme. Projects and programmes may fall under the SWAp umbrella.

The introduction of the sector-wide-approach did not bring an end to the project or programme approaches to development. Whatever shape projects take, they exist alongside the sectoral approach and may be expected to (1) lead to experiments with innovative approaches going beyond the competence of the national government; (2) serve regions and/or groups beyond the reach of the national governmental services; (3) offer technical aid in the field of capacity building (education and training); and (4) contribute to institutional strengthening, 'good governance' and more democratic decision making.

Because the project approach as a support modality has its own unique characteristics, there will be a continuing need for this approach in the decades to come.

Conventional development planning and management processes

A project or programme can be considered to be any series of activities and tasks that: (1) have a specific objective to be completed within certain specifications; (2) have defined start and end dates; (3) have funding limits (if applicable); and

(4) consume resources (money, people, equipment). Project planning consists of the planning, organising, directing, and controlling of resources for a relatively short period of time. It is established in order to meet specific goals and objectives. One of the devices helpful when dealing with project planning is the logical framework.

Logical framework

Logical framework (log-frame) was developed in the USA during the early 1970s and has been used by a variety of development agencies ever since. It developed and combined analysis and *visualisation* techniques enabling a systematic and logical setting out of the project/programme's objectives and their causal relationships, in order to indicate how to check whether these objectives have been achieved and to establish which assumptions outside the project/programme's scope may influence its success.

Since 1984 this goal- or objective-oriented planning system has been the official system of a leading donor agency in development cooperation, the German Technical Cooperation (GTZ).[59] Other organisations adopted it towards the end of the 1980s. From the start of the 1990s, applications of the logical framework have faced mounting criticism. Many stakeholders find log frames to be alien and illogical, primarily because they exclude the logic of primary stakeholders.

Ultimately this criticism called for revising the model. The new, more flexible and reformed log-frame was called the Project Cycle Management (PCM) and has been employed all over the world ever since, within the context of major development operations involving financing and training.

The main results of this process of Project Cycle Management (PCM) are summarised in a matrix (a visualisation of the logical framework) depicting a project's or programme's most important aspects within a logical format. Such a framework can prove useful, depending upon the degree of responsiveness it allows. A log-frame is an instrument by means of which the project team may discuss the progress made. It visualises the logic of the development intervention step-by-step.

Project Cycle Management: the integrated approach

The integrated approach is a method for managing a project cycle's six phases by means of an analysis of the most important elements of each phase and the criteria for cohesion and sustainability applicable throughout. Figure 7.1 indicates that preparation, implementation and evaluation are not successive phases in the life of a project or programme. These functions are simultaneously operational, although one or the other will dominate at any given time according to the manner in which the situation develops.

The relationship between the six phases is not necessarily linear. The created cycle is one in which each phase is fed by the previous one. Identification, for example, can be performed correctly only on the basis of an evaluation of the previous steps. Moreover, evaluation and monitoring procedures are liable to lead to a new identification phase entailing reprogramming or programming amendments.

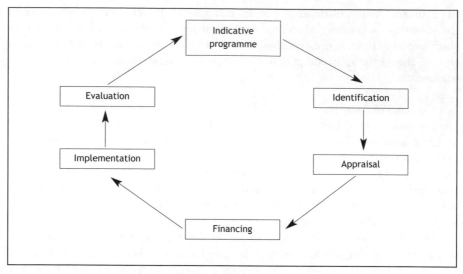

Figure 7.1 The six phases of the project cycle

PCM involves research activities in all phases so as to take informed decisions throughout the process. A complete range of research modalities and instruments are applied. For a systemic overview of the research instruments applied in the various phases see Appendix 2.

8

Assessing the Results of Development Activities

How can the results of development activities (workshops, performances, projects or programmes) be assessed?

Monitoring and evaluation

The difference between monitoring and evaluation might be formulated as follows: if monitoring is primarily concerned with issues and production processes, evaluation focuses on the effects and impacts of development projects. Research activities form part of the project cycle's phases. In the course of this process, monitoring (as an integral part of project implementation) and evaluation are key features of a well-run project or programme, and should be included in the proposal from the outset.

Monitoring 'enables observation of the project's implementation in relation to institutional responsibilities, the objectives set, participation, emerging changes and the likelihood of attaining planned results' (UNESCO, 2001: 86). *Evaluation* enables the judgement of a project/programme's value. For that purpose, the evaluator requires (1) to be informed about the project/programme regarding what has occurred, or is occurring; (2) to compare a project/programme's actual results with its planned/initial objectives in order to see if these objectives were reached; and (3) to present an opinion on whether or not there is value in what has occurred.

A distinction has to be made between the *ex ante* and the *ex post* evaluation.[60] According to De Hegedus (1995: 67) it is important to underscore the relevance of an evaluation conducted before completing the project (*ex ante*). Such information facilitates further planning and maximises the chances of successful intervention. By systemising data on similar experiences (evaluation at the end of the project), the parties involved provide themselves with useful information in order to support other projects. This *ex-post* evaluation can be used to carry out in-depth studies on a project's impact and outcomes.

Baseline surveys and benchmarking studies

The benchmarking process is a research technique which has proved to be remarkably useful in the service industry. A benchmark is a standard of excellence or achievement employed to compare and measure similar items. It is a technique for identifying measurable successes ('best practices')[61] of others and applying them to one's own organisation. The benchmarking process compares an organisation's practices, processes and outcomes with standards of excellence in order to help identify and plan one's own programme possibilities and to identify those one would like to match or exceed.

Therefore, every project or programme has to start with a proper baseline survey and needs assessment to be able to benchmark the effects aimed for by the intervention. It is otherwise impossible to measure results in terms of behavioural changes or attitudes. Both the baseline survey and the needs assessment are necessary in order to establish the knowledge, attitudes and practices of the intended target audience. This will provide a basis for further impact assessments by means of social surveys.

Measuring impact

Engaged in the professionalisation process, development practitioners became preoccupied with measuring the impact of their work. The impact of an intervention is the sum total of its positive as well as negative, intended and unintended, long-term effects. Through measuring this impact an organisation or donor seeks to find out how effective the intervention has been. This is done by studying the outcomes – the results achieved at the end of the process. Assessing the impact forms part of the continuous evaluation process.

A distinction has to be made between measuring short-term and long-term effectiveness:

Short-term effectiveness is measured by the degree to which participants identify with a project and accept it as their own. This is regarded as an indication of the level of participation achieved. *Long-term effectiveness* is measured after several months or even after two to four years. Assessing long-term effectiveness in terms of the sustainability and impact of development interventions is often very difficult. The results of such exercises are open to debate. The economic return on the investments may turn out to be too modest for some donor agencies. Nevertheless, indications may be given as to how project results can be continued and which environment offers the best opportunities for sustaining the results obtained.

Indicators

Indicators are increasingly standardised means through which the goals and outputs of a project, a programme or a sector are measured and given a specific meaning. Indicators provide clear signals of success (or failure) and a 'quality standard' for a project or programme. An indicator should provide, where possible, a clearly defined unit of measurement and a target, detailing means of verification and specifying the expected source of the information. Well-defined indicators are simple, providing the needed information in a wink. An example from everyday life is the petrol gauge on a car dashboard.

However, other instruments also inform the researcher of achievements and test results. In a training context, indicators refer to the information needed in order to determine progress during the training and at the conclusion (monitoring and evaluation), towards meeting stated training objectives. The outcomes of exams and tests measure the indicators of learning achievements. Laughter, applause, offering money or hissing have long been used as indicators of the success of a theatrical performance.

Indicators are also applied in national surveys. The purpose of these surveys is to measure development in terms of production and national income. Indicators attempt to reconcile two requirements: to be concrete and quantifiable, on the one hand, and to represent important, decisive aspects of the cultural process on the other. A very concrete and quantifiable indicator in almost all rural societies is access to land. This is considered a crucial indicator of the well-being and social status of its citizens.

Less concrete and more difficult to measure are abstract notions such as (the increasing degree of) equity, empowerment, participation and sustainability. A problem with empowerment is that it cannot be measured easily at the end of a development intervention.

The growing importance of indicators raises the question of how agents select and apply them, whether in fact they reflect the phenomena analysed, and how accurate they are. Indicators often provide only partial information, mostly masking major disparities, which in fact form the quintessence in diagnosing the cultural system's condition.

Human development indicators

Human development is a process of enlarging people's choices, of enhancing their effective freedom to pursue whatever they have reason to value. As a consequence, human development indicators, essentially economic in nature at first, now cover broad aspects of life which come into play with (cultural) development.

The level of (cultural) development is measured both in terms of input indicators (resource allocation) as well as output indicators (outcomes and achievements). The input indicators refer to the process of cultural development, reflecting upon resources (human capital, time investment) going into the process of development, and hence are amenable to policies. Input indicators reflect expenditures on development. The input of resources generates output in terms of products and activities measurable in terms of amount and increase.

The output can be measured in terms of the number of items produced or their monetary value. In the cultural sector we have the annual number of new book titles (and copies per edition) produced and on the consumption side we have the number of titles sold that particular year. Other examples are the sales of music albums, annual cinema sales, kilograms *per capita* of paper consumed.

Thus for TfD one can measure the quantity of the courses, workshops and/or performances on offer and the number of successful participants. One can measure the increased knowledge of the participants or the acquisition of skills. By means of *tracer studies*[62] it is possible to find out how this knowledge and these skills have affected people's lives for the better. The activities a project develops (such as training courses, workshops or curriculum development) are an indication of the degree of participation.

Indicators of successful 'empowerment'

Because empowerment strives at improving the capacity of people to organise themselves in order to participate actively and effectively in a changing environment, the impact of empowerment will only become noticeable within the learners' social context some time after they receive the training. Indicators may be employed, however, in order to provide some indication of successful empowerment. Some indicators for recognising the achievement of empowerment are:

At the level of the individual:
• participation in crucial decision-making processes;
• expansion of a person's worldview or cultural understanding;
• strengthening of a person's 'voice' so that he or she has the courage to participate in dialogue or even break down the dominant discursive forms;
• broadening of the field of social identities or roles;
• achieving more responsibility as participants over projects/programmes;
• degree of ownership of resources;
• capacity to cope with change;
• gaining of positions in the community (or society at large), hitherto not held.

At the level of the community:
• increasing participation in existing organisational structures;
• growing capacity to change organisational structures;
• growing number of new initiatives taken by participants in the learning process;
• increasing degree of sustainable self-organisation (individual or group-based);
• increased number of actions taken to improve the position of the poor and underprivileged.

At the national level:
• awareness of social and political rights;
• integration in national development plans;
• existence of networks and publications;
• growing attention in the media.

Cultural indicators of development

Are culture and statistics still the sworn enemies they were long considered to be? Is having a keen eye for statistics worthwhile even in the cultural sector ? If our understanding of culture under globalisation is to be advanced on an empirical basis, we must underline the need for cultural indicators and their aggregates in order to contribute useful information on the cultural sector.

As long as cultural phenomena are measurable in terms of data (numbers, presence or absence, preferences, expenditure) it is possible to establish cultural indicators for development.

A practical integration of culture in development requires reliable statistical data, too. Such statistics offer us a better understanding of development and investment trends within the cultural sector and of the consumption of cultural goods and services. This new knowledge should be developed through the exchange of information between governments, the cultural industries sector and civil society (Klamer, 1996: 27).

During the UNESCO Workshop on Cultural Indicators of Development (January 1996), the idea was introduced of using time as a basis for several indicators. For example, reading books, newspapers and journals could be measured by the time spent, as could the consumption of music, film or opera. Education could also be assessed in terms of the average number of years spent in schools and colleges.

However, an exclusive focus on consumption would neglect an important dimension, namely creativity. In terms of quantitative output figures, a distinction has to be made between people systematically trained to work and *produce* in the cultural sector and the people who *consume* products and arts in the cultural sector. In this context participation is often as much about production as consumption (McKinley, 1998: 325).

9

TfD and Development Support Communication

'Theatre, puppets, dance and music are firmly rooted in the traditional cultural and artistic expressions of many communities in poorer countries. It is difficult to imagine a community that has completely forgotten any of these forms of collective participation and entertainment.' (Dagrón, 2001: 24–5)

How does TfD relate to development support communication strategies?

Development support communication

In the widest sense communication is a term for the structured dynamic processes relating to the interconnectedness of living systems. In the context of development support communication, however, communication refers to a public exchange through which the production of knowledge can be monitored in order to promote and support development programmes based on participation. One of the tasks of development support communication is to stimulate, sustain and increase the capacity of people to know how to think, how to work and how to solve problems. The aim is a better quality of life, resting on an enhanced potential for developing individuals, families, communities and the nation as a whole more effectively.

To perform this task, a mix of communication styles and channels is applied, including entertainment, news, information, advocacy, community action, written materials, drama, organisational partnerships, peer support, public meetings, investigative journalism, and many others. All kinds of popular media are involved: the printed and the electronic as well as local media and means of expression such as traditional tales, plays, proverbs, dances and songs.

Before deciding to adopt a development support communication strategy one must map the communication and information environment of the geographic area in which one plans to work by means of a survey. The communication and information environment consists of each and every opportunity for information and communication existing within a community. Members of the community have different degrees of access to these opportunities, depending on their income, physical environment, educational level and alertness.

The information and communication environment covers all general-purpose and general-interest information, including educational and entertainment programmes disseminated through radio, television and other audio-visual media as well as stories and messages communicated by family members or other people, printed media (books, rural newspapers, magazines, recipes) and audio tapes. Thus, in mapping the information and communication environment, attention is paid not only to the electronic and conventional printed media at national level, but also to popular media and oral tradition genres at local level, including personal face-to-face communication.[63]

All these media can be distinguished into two main categories: one-way and two-way flows of communication. *One-way-flows of communication* include written materials (notes, reports, manuals, brochures, leaflets, books, press releases, advertisements, newspaper articles, newsletters) and audio-visual materials (radio/television programmes, videos, films, slide shows, computer presentations, CD roms, webpages). *Two-way flows of communication* involve an exchange of information, by means of an interaction process through which persons or groups relate to each other in sharing information, culture and experiences. Such exchanges include person-to-person communication (discussions, meetings, working groups, steering committees, workshops, seminars, conferences, letters, e-mails, public information desks/centres, telephone info-desks) and participatory communication tools (focus group discussions, problem tree development, preparation of action plans, theatre, role play).

Communication model

One of the most common models used in scientific research into communication is still the sender–receiver dyad.[64] Several critical comments have been made on the application of this model. One is that it is rather sender-focused. Most studies using this model concentrated on the source of information, the message as designed by the sender.[65] In the course of the interaction between sender and receiver the model starts off with the sender dominating the communication process, not paying enough attention to the feedback loop from the receiver, nor to the possibility of interactive and interchangeable roles for senders and receivers.

Another comment on this model is that it is inappropriate to use a simple linear model of communication involving individual senders and receivers in order to explain complicated processes of social change. To come up with plausible explanations of social change, a model of communication is required which is cyclical and relational and leads to an outcome of mutual exchange rather than one-sided, individual change.

In response to this criticism scientists began to concentrate on studying the ways messages are received and interpreted by audiences (McQuail, 1997). This model is rooted in the idea of feedback: performers (teachers or actors) are involved in a dynamic process or system within which they are seen to react and adapt. Since the 1970s these theories have been known as 'reception theories'. Cultural studies of media consumers aim to understand the power dynamics of media systems, the role media play in people's everyday lives, and the particular nature of audience experience.

An advantage of this model is: it applies to all performative communication processes, including theatre and education. Within this context, 'theatre' is taken to refer to the complex of phenomena associated with the performer–audience transaction, to what takes place between and among performers and spectators. The performers, together with the playwright, choreographer, stage director, producer and other actors are conceived as 'the senders'.

The same applies to the educator–learner interaction. Education is a performative process, involving the establishment of a common framework, the assumption of roles, dialogue and reciprocal processes of learning and teaching. Within the educational context the sender consists of the teacher, coach, facilitator or any designer of educational tools such as slides, video, film or distance education programme. Whatever their performance, the relationship will be direct and face-to-face, based on oral expression.

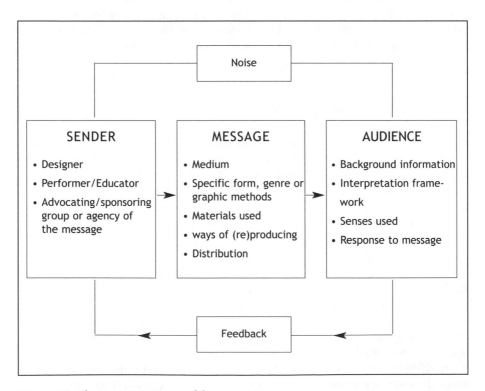

Figure 9.1 The communication model

Communication and social change

According to a Rockefeller Foundation position paper (1999: 11–12) communication programmes have, very simplistically, tended to fulfil three roles in development thinking and practice:

1 To inform and persuade people to adopt certain behaviours and practices beneficial to them; for example, to urge them to have fewer children and inform them how to do so.
2 To enhance the image and profile of the work of organisations involved in development with a view to boosting the credibility of their work, raising more funding and generally improving public perceptions.
3 To enable community consultation over specific initiatives on a more targeted level within communities.

Access to communication and information is a precondition of ownership. A communication process owned by the people provides the community members with equal opportunities regarding participation in development.

Participation in development can only be increased when communication systems start serving the needs of the vast majority in the rural rather than in the urban areas. TfD is a good option to make this happen. Many observers and researchers stress that there is no guarantee that greater access to information will automatically lead to increased participation in development.

The arts are a major form of human communication and expression. Individuals and groups apply them to explore, express and communicate ideas, feelings and experiences. Artistic works can inform, teach, persuade and provoke thought. They can reproduce and reinforce existing ideas and values, challenge them, or offer new ways of thinking and feeling. They can confirm existing values and practices, and they can bring about change. As a result, the arts play an important role in shaping people's understanding of themselves as individuals and members of society, as well as their understanding of the world in which they live.

Conventional printed media

Conventional printed media such as books, newspapers, magazines, leaflets, brochures, comics and posters, thanks to printing and duplicating techniques, are capable of existing on their own, independently of those who produced them initially. For that reason they have the potential to be disseminated *en masse*.

In general, national governments as well as the adult population hold the view that 'books feed the mind'. People at all levels of society generally verbalise a very strong positive attitude towards reading. In most nations, however, developing and developed alike, one observes poorly developed reading habits at all levels. The contradiction between a positive attitude towards reading and poor reading behaviour in practice usually has to do with limited financial resources being available for buying reading materials and with priorities when it comes to spending limited free time.

Newspapers probably supply the most important reading material for adults, followed by magazines and then books. In regions with little cash income, a copy of a single newspaper may be passed from hand to hand, not purchased hot from the press. Local newspapers – including photographs, folklore, poetry and short stories – are apparently most popular in rural areas. They have proved to be a strong tool in development support communication at local level.

Apart from books, newspapers and magazines, popular novellas and comics are in demand in urban as well as rural environments. Broad layers of the public, young and old, read them. So far, however, no proof has been found that they strengthen development communication – although comics and photo-novels may be effective in campaigning and in simple information leaflets.

Radio and television

The radio is the single medium in developing countries ultimately suitable for nation-wide promotional purposes and has, in fact, become the oral medium of modern times. In some parts of the world it is still very strong and popular, offering a two-way mode of communication with the power to integrate education and entertainment. Radio has the potential to reach all inhabited regions: the islands of the Caribbean and the Pacific, but also the inland areas of Africa and Central America (Musa 1998: 146). Radio drama is very popular in West Africa. Even if rural communities and marginal slums have no electricity, radio remains important and influential there, thanks to its low cost and accessibility.

Regional relay stations are especially important, often addressing the population in its local language while airing the local music. Radio is thus a success factor in development support communication. It has motivated and stimulated people to take part in campaign-like activities, although it also seems to lend itself to providing more elaborate background information.

From the early 1960s onwards Everett M. Rogers has experimented with communication strategies for social change. Starting his career with a social engineering perspective, he slowly evolved a participatory approach to development. Rogers first introduced this more persuasive way of communicating development-related messages in his book *Communication of Innovation* (1962). It fitted into the early thinking of 'development studies', in which social scientists tried to figure out how to implement simple 'modernisation' approaches towards development. Rogers presented his theory on the dissemination of new ideas and practices as a crucial component in the process of modernisation. Later on he developed a marketing approach to communication.[66]

In the late 1980s, together with Arvind Singhal, Rogers developed another approach which they referred to as 'entertainment-education', a communication strategy for social change to achieve development goals.[67] 'Entertainment-

---

Box 9.1 Training television soap scriptwriters (1991)

In November 1991 UNICEF organised a workshop in Rio de Janeiro,[70] involving eighteen writers from seven Central American countries and the USA, to explore opportunities of broadcasting *telenovelas* that would introduce audiences to new ways of looking at human survival, street children and education. After returning to their countries a number of these scriptwriters started to express their newly acquired insights:

- José Ignacio Cabrujas wrote *El Paseo de la Gracia de Dios*, a Venezuelan series relating of the lives of the inhabitants of a particular traditional street in Caracas including (in a very casual way) subjects such as health problems and child feeding in the dialogue and social interaction between the characters.
- Sergio Vainman wrote *La Banda del Golden Rocket*, a *telenovela* from Argentina for young people including messages about themes like AIDS prevention and drug addiction.

Another television scriptwriter taking part in this workshop was Miguel Sabido from Mexico, who earlier had developed several soap series for Televisa in Mexico for purposes of social development. In fact, Televisa was one of the first production companies to experiment with *telenovelas* that were not only entertaining but also meant to educate. One such soap focused on stimulating attendance at literacy classes, telling the story of a grandfather who wanted to learn how to read a story to his grandson. After this touching episode the subscription to literacy courses increased by 60 per cent.

Educational soaps produced by Televisa include: *Ven Conmigo* (Come with Me), intended to stimulate literacy; *Acompaname* (Accompany Me), in support of family planning; *Vamos Juntos* (Let's Go Together), encouraging better treatment of children; and *Nosotros las Mujeres* (We, Women), to improve the societal status of Mexican women.

In the educational *telenovela*, almost all leading female characters experience a change in their life. From the moment they become aware of the importance of the social theme, they develop into independent women who no longer want to conform automatically to the rules of male-dominated 'malestream' society (Dubbelboer and Paulissen, 1995: 75–91).

---

education' explores the process of designing and implementing a media message to both entertain and educate, thereby increasing knowledge of an educational issue, creating favourable attitudes, and changing overt behaviour. One of the media formats of 'entertainment-education' is the soap opera. Culturally sensitive radio and TV soap operas are, for example, produced within the field of population education.[65]

Today, television 'soaps' are a worldwide phenomenon. Touching upon love, sex, money and power, the genre has been referred to as modern popular theatre, viewing society through a looking glass while focusing on the ambitions and dreams people have on the difference between good and evil, the hesitation between ideals and pragmatism.

Central America and the Indian subcontinent are now world leaders in the exploitation of this melodramatic genre. Apart from the leading producers in the USA and Australia, Mexico and Brazil are considered to be important soap producers and exporters. Other regions such as Egypt, Indonesia, Ghana and South Africa[69] have begun producing local soaps too. The problems presented in these series are mostly of a country-specific nature.

Initially, during the 1970s, soap production and consumption was severely criticised by intellectuals and communication experts, because the soap characters were considered to present the viewer with over-simplified role models. However, because of strong identification with the characters and the soap's appeal to a mass audience, it came to serve purposes of social development such as improving child care, nutrition, hygiene and sanitation.

In the course of the 1980s soaps were developed not only to entertain but also to inform and educate. The most renowned experimental programmes were produced in Central America and India. Because family life is a core aspect of soaps, they are perfectly suited to portraying certain relationships, particularly between men and women (gender) and between young and old (the generation gap). The gender theme was used to explore sexuality, birth control and AIDS prevention. The generation gap theme explored the principles and values applied in raising children; the necessity of literacy, basic knowledge and skills; and the value of education in general ('our future lies in the hands of our children').

Especially in Mexico and Brazil soaps (*telenovelas*) were experimented with as a means of development support communication, presenting themes such as drug addiction, AIDS prevention, physical violence against children, alcoholism, the new role of women in contemporary society and many other aspects of daily urban existence during the 1990s.

Multi-media campaigning: buying the product

Campaigning is a systematic means of communicating information on a major (national) issue to large numbers of people. The primary aim of campaign-like activities is to promote awareness and to help people understand major issues, policies or programmes.

A campaign has a sense of urgency about it. It is only effective if one experiences the subject as 'hot': 'This is what we need to do – and we need to do it now!' In order to emphasise the sense of urgency metaphors are used. A literacy campaign during the 1960s and 1970s, for example, was often an 'expedition', a 'fight', or even a 'crusade'. Another example is the 'war against hunger', an action programme in poverty alleviation. These metaphors strengthen the event's organisational imagery. The use of life drama and music emphasise this 'here and now' urgency.

Organising campaign-like activities requires a collaborative media effort. While person-to-person live theatre is the most effective way of getting a message across, sometimes a demand for other media exists. In addition to the plays, books, radio programmes and videos (using live actors and puppets) have been produced in order to reach a wider segment of the public.

Short-term campaigns are easier to organise and initially attract a much larger audience. Even better are repetitive campaign-like activities, used as reminders of the campaign objectives. Campaigning programmes may last from five to ten weeks. Follow-ups can be undertaken by a network of fieldworkers/facilitators (information officers) supporting local people (in learning groups).

Although campaigns have been shown to be very effective in short-term mobilisation of resources, emphasis has shifted from persuasion[71] through the transmission of information by outside technical experts to dialogue, debate and negotiation on issues important to members of the community.

10
Non-formal Education

Where does TfD fit in the educational system?

Within the educational sector a distinction is made between formal, non-formal and informal education. All three types of education form part of and contribute to a permanent process of continuing education or life-long learning, and are, therefore, considered to be mutually supportive rather than competitive. Definitions of these three types of education have been offered in Chapter 3 (see Box 3.1, 'The educational landscape', p. 45).

In practice, however, it is quite difficult to maintain the distinction between formal, non-formal and informal learning: most schooling includes a broader educative function as well, whereas a school-like transfer of knowledge and skills can be detected in informal learning situations.

The need for non-formal education gradually evolved because many children and young adults were not able to follow all successive phases of formal education. In many developing countries, only half of those enrolled in first grade complete the cycle of five or six years. The problem of students prematurely leaving school often results in a certain degree of illiteracy amongst drop-outs. In fact, between 20 per cent and 40 per cent of the entire education budget is spent on youngsters who do not remain in the system (Banya and Elu, 1997: 483–4).

As in the formal school system, non-formal education appears to empower participants through a social learning process: they acquire new knowledge and skills and the sense of confidence necessary to adopt new ways of behaving such as group formation, decision-making and leadership skills.

Whatever the specific objectives, the basic idea of non-formal education programmes is that the learners should be stimulated to improve their circumstances through their own efforts, and that the acquisition of new knowledge and skills plays an essential part in this. Learning groups are set up within which skills are acquired that may help to solve problems regarded as important by the members of the community.

Within the community the school, as an institution, exclusively aims at the acquisition and transfer of a certain curriculum of knowledge and skills. Figure 10.1 provides a schematic impression of the links between formal and non-formal education within the learning environment at national and community levels. In this context the learning environment may be described as each and every opportunity towards education and information existing within a community which the people use, and to which they have a degree of access dependent on their income, physical environment, educational level and alertness to topics of interest.

Adult education

In 1997 the Fifth World Conference on Adult Education (CONFINTEA V) was held in Hamburg. In the context of the Hamburg Declaration, adult education denotes the entire body of ongoing learning processes, formal or otherwise, whereby people regarded as adults by the society to which they belong develop their abilities, enrich their knowledge, improve their technical or professional qualifications, or turn them in a new direction in order to meet their own needs and those of their society.

In other words, adult education is considered to be a special form of non-formal education, targeted at a variety of adult audiences and entangled with rapid societal change. Adult education/training is the most important instrument or cornerstone in non-formal education, providing tools to change the socio-economic expectations by teaching new skills. Distinctions can be drawn between adult education variously aimed at:

* *training literacy skills:* involving reading and writing skills and simple techniques of calculating (numeracy); also referred to as the three R's: reading, writing and arithmetic;
* *training technical and/or vocational skills:* improving the status of disadvantaged people and introducing special methods of vocationalised learning;
* *promoting and empowering behavioural changes* in order to improve the quality of life (health, agriculture, sanitation, mother and child care, nutrition and other developmental concerns).

Adult learning has the following characteristics:

* it is learner-centred: adults learn what is of interest to them and what has become meaningful to them;
* it contributes to making the lives of the learners more meaningful (for example, in terms of increased self-esteem and/or skills acquired);
* it is experiential learning: solutions come from personal understanding and are congruent with life experiences;
* it is an active, practical tuition with the focus on applying the knowledge and skills acquired;

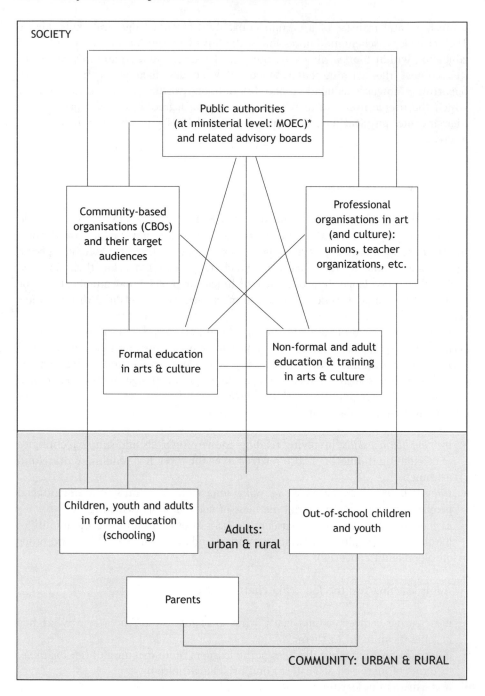

Figure 10.1 Linking formal and non-formal education at national and local levels
* MOEC: Ministry of Education and Culture

- it leads to a future-oriented vision of life, motivating further self-learning;
- it shows results within a reasonable timeframe (measurable in a range of positive changes such as skills, income, knowledge, safe drinking water, or the cure of diarrhoea);
- it is a social process: learning takes place in groups, presenting the opportunity to participate actively in the (inter-)learning process by exchanging ideas, self-expression and learning from others.

Obviously, given its origin and characteristics, TfD is closely related to adult education, especially when used as a process.

NGOs most often provide adult education in the form of 'crash courses': short-term, practical-skills training courses. As adult education is perceived as a social learning event, attention is paid to creating an enabling learning environment by (1) introducing participatory training methods; (2) stimulating community involvement and participation; (3) changing the recipe approach to a partnership approach; (4) working closely with other stakeholders within the country; and (5) relating the teaching of literacy skills to income-generating skills training.

Various views on adult education are held. On the one hand, the managerial view perceives adult education as human resource development. On the other hand, adult education can be seen as an instrument for democratisation, empowering people to organise themselves. Properly planned and organised, adult education is a strategy for managing economic and political change, and helping individuals cope with it.

11

The Importance
of Art Education

'Culture is a low priority for most modern governments (though in the past it was often second to defence).' (Mundy, 2000: 12)

What is the importance of art education for society?

Aims of art education

Nations have long understood that education is an essential dimension of cultural development. A school curriculum is a selection from the knowledge, skills and traditions of a given culture. (Council of Europe, 1997: 43).

Education has a crucial role to play in providing participants with the knowledge and skills necessary to change their own socio-economic prospects and those of the larger community of which they are a part. Schools are responsible for enabling young people to gain aesthetic experience and develop expressive skills. Students can also gain in terms of social and personal learning, using the arts as a medium to explore and learn in other areas of the curriculum.

Institutions such as the national school system have played a very important role as an instrument of cultural intervention; and as such of normalising knowledge, skills, common standards for 'good taste' and the appreciation of the arts and national culture (Kloos, 1995: 36). In general, this part of school education is referred to as the educational system's hidden curriculum, the implicit and self-evident values underlying a written curriculum and not directly recognisable as a message.

In the early 1980s Rosenblum (1981) argued that popular arts should be included in the arts curriculum for a variety of reasons: (1) popular arts facilitate the aesthetic experience; (2) their content is of relevance to the students and this, with the help of art criticism, can lead to a more critical analysis of these and other art forms; (3) popular arts allow students to discuss matters that engage them emotionally; (4) popular arts can aid a student's understanding of his or her

Box 11.1 School theatre in Sierra Leone during the 1970s and 1980s

Sierra Leone became an independent nation in 1961. Between 1991 and 1996 it went through a civil war followed by ongoing armed conflicts. The educational system in Sierra Leone is a copy of the British system. The content of the curriculum and syllabus of this educational system has not been Africanised to any significant degree. The syllabus in arts and literature is still based on the Western canon of literature. There are more foreign than African texts on the reading list. According to Wright (1994: 179) theatre in Sierra Leone exists in three basic forms: (1) traditional performing arts of high aesthetic value that include African forms of storytelling, celebratory dances and the performances of the exclusively male or female (secret) societies, all having a social function within rural communities; (2) plays forming part of literary drama, being the products of many international playwrights, African and foreign alike; and (3) popular theatre, locally written plays dealing with contemporary local themes, and written in Krio (the nation's *lingua franca*).

An intersection between school and theatre had already been created during the early 1970s by the organisation of inter-school drama competitions in Freetown. Although theatre was considered an extra-curricular activity, these competitions initiated a surge of youthful interest in drama, especially because it created intense rivalries between schools.

'These annual competitions sparked many students' interest in acting and the theatre in general. Students who did not take part in the productions attended in thousands to watch. Three semi-professional theatre companies went talent scouting at the inter- and intra-school competitions and by the late 1970s students were working backstage and appearing (even in leading roles) in the productions of Tabule Experimental Theatre, the African Heritage Workshop and Songhai Theatre. This development attracted droves of young people as well as adults to theatre audiences' (Wright, 1994: 179).

These performances were so popular because the performers spoke Krio and the plays touched upon local problems, depicted characters recognisable to the audience and portrayed familiar situations. In this way school theatre contributed to a genuine revival of popular theatre in Sierra Leone. During the mid-1980s, however, this form of theatre waned: no new theatre companies emerged; actors were leaving, and the low ticket prices were still too expensive for the commoner. People could not afford to go to the theatre.

culture, as well as the cultures of other peoples; and (5) popular arts can provide the art curriculum with topics of great social relevance.

Through participation in art programmes, pupils learn to understand the arts as a family of related ways of knowing and communicating. Learning in the arts is an active as well as an interactive and experiential process:

1 An *active process*: Pupils learn to make sense of their experiences and construct a range of critical *frameworks*. These frameworks allow them, on the one hand, to use the concepts of aesthetic understanding and practice; and, on the other, to make judgements on the effectiveness and impact of works of art. For example, one learns to describe and judge what one sees and feels using more formal processes – such as writing reviews or analyses and making reports – to describe, analyse, interpret and evaluate experiences.
2 An *interactive process*: Art education should be perceived not as an isolated element within the curriculum, but as an interactive part of the individual's entire education. A pupil participates in his or her own creative activity while understanding and engaging with the artistic, cultural and intellectual work of others – learning to respect their needs, rights[72] and (aesthetic) values.
3 An *experiential process*: Students learn through sensory perceptions and observations. They use their senses, perceptions, feelings, values and knowledge to communicate through the arts. Through this expression they come to a better understanding of their physical world and make appropriate choices concerning it.

Learning in the arts involves developing skills across a wide range of human activities: verbal and physical skills; logical and intuitive thinking; and spatial, rhythmic, visual and kinaesthetic awareness. Learning in the arts often involves integrating skills from different areas of human potentiality, promoting multi-sensory learning.

Within the curriculum, 'art education' aims at personality development, the transfer of knowledge and the release of creativity in order to contribute to optimal individual participation within the context of societal and cultural life at large (Demirbas and Rabbae, 1990: 13).

According to Bastos Barbosa (1992: 6) one of the main functions of art education is to mediate between art and the general public. Art education goes thus beyond the curriculum of formal schooling. It also forms part of the general provision of arts education in the field of *non-formal and adult education* constituted by the media, museums and various cultural centres. Such institutions ensure that art is no longer a commodity for an economically privileged and well-educated minority of people.

The curriculum

In developing an endogenous artistic environment, most ministries of education and culture organise the arts at two levels: the artistic-promotional and the educational level. The Department of Education is responsible for organising and training artistic potential by means of including the arts and fine arts within the curriculum of the formal educational system.

Art education has two components: the appreciative and the creative. Creation concerns the making of art in an active way by acquisition of skills, whilst appreciation is concerned with the understanding and analysis of works of art. The creative skills acquired by professionals and non-professionals result in artistic expression and production (including design). Appreciation of art has two modes: the receptive mode (aesthetic perception) when one views art in a museum, listens to a concert or attends a play; and the critical mode, when one studies or reflects upon the arts.

The art curriculum in the formal education system has been developed on the basis of four interrelated domains that yield a quadrant of major learning outcomes:

* Learners generate art works that communicate ideas;
* Learners use the skills, techniques, processes, conventions and technologies of the arts;
* Learners use their aesthetic understanding to respond to, reflect on and evaluate the arts;
* Learners understand the role of the arts in society.

Distinctions between creation and appreciation of the arts by professionals and non-professionals have been presented in Table 11.1, although the table does not depict the necessary overlap between the domains in the quadrant.

In teaching students how to appreciate art and artefacts, the main principles to be dealt with are: *discrimination* and *interpretation*. Students learn to describe and reason about patterns, structures and relationships in order to understand, interpret, justify and predict. Students become familiar with how conventions in the arts develop and change, both over time and within particular cultures. They learn to value, evaluate, challenge, discriminate, feel, respond and enjoy the arts as a whole.

Enjoying art brings along with it the necessary knowledge and skills to evaluate it. There are several ways to do this. Students must learn to distinguish art objects belonging to various periods and regions. One approach is to find indications regarding the timeframe in which the work of art was produced. Another is to find out more about the 'school' or movement to which the artist belonged or, on the contrary, did not belong. Or, one might compare it with art produced by other artists from the same period in order to see if similarities in style or theme exist. After some training this enables a genre evaluation.

According to Hall (1969: 81), the study of the art of the past makes it possible to learn a little about how humans respond to the nature and organisation of visual systems and expectations. In this way, he argues, one can deduce what the perceptual world of early man may have looked like. Thus the basic capability of discriminating and comparing acquired through art education can provide the basis for a deeper perspective.

Table 11.1 Appreciation of the arts by professionals and non-professionals

	Creation	**Appreciation**
Professional	Learners generate art works that communicate ideas. (Artists, designers)	Learners understand the role of arts in society. Skills for decodification, understanding and evaluation of works of art, etc. Studying and reflecting upon arts. Analysis of artistic works. Essay writing on the arts. Personal accounts of experiencing the arts. (Art critics, historians, trend watchers)
Non-professional	Learners develop creative ways of expressing themselves. Experiencing the arts. Learners use the skills, techniques, processes, conventions and technologies of the arts. (Art lovers, amateurs, leisure time course participants in the arts)	Learners use their aesthetic understanding to respond to, reflect on and evaluate art. Acquired knowledge enables learners to make their own preferences and choices, either in music, drama or the visual arts. (Art consumers: visitors of museums, concerts, art galleries, theatre plays, etc.)

Confronted with a work of art, each individual will experience something very directly, but not necessarily because it appeals to his/her feelings. First of all, according to Crego and Groot (1985: 224), those unfamiliar with mainstream art, who rarely visit a museum or a theatre, will look at a work of art as a puzzle, trying to find significance in it by comparing it with other art forms with which they are familiar or with matters in their daily experience to which the work of art might refer. Realism and recognition are important evaluative criteria.

As is already clear from this statement, differences in art appreciation are directly related to social differences. Schooling, training and a positive attitude towards works of art in the home environment are of great help in learning to evaluate art. To be able to discuss the meaning of art has become a symbol of distinction in itself. In brief, knowledge of culture and art is related to the social environment in which one grows up. Cultural resources in the parental family influence the level of education and of cultural participation.

Box 11.2 NGO initiates art education in India

In 1949 Mrinalini Sarabhai formed the dance group Darpana and a school to train classical dancers: the Darpana Academy of Performing Arts, based in Ahmedabad. It has various departments: dance, drama, puppetry, and one called Janavak (see below). Dance training is mainly provided for students who aim to become members of the Darpana Dance Company, made up of young women and men trained in Bharatanatyam, Kuchipudi and Kathakali, most of them soloists in their own right. The company's repertoire is very wide, ranging from the traditional to the contemporary, from the classical to the abstract. Individual dancers are also trained to take workshops and lecture demonstrations.

The first initiative to create a Drama Department goes back to 1959, when the Darpana group pioneered Gujarati experimental theatre, emphasising the production of offbeat original plays by playwrights who now enjoy a national standing.

Since 1967, the Puppetry Department of the Darpana group has worked with many kinds of puppets, participating for many years in the revival of the ancient form of leather shadow puppets from Andhra. The group aims to entertain as well as present development-oriented themes. It also creates special programmes for government and local agencies. With teachers, children, government workers, rural health workers and other specialised groups, it conducts workshops in order to teach the effective use of puppetry for communication.

Darpana's latest initiative is a special department called into being in 1982. It is called Janavak and aims for the revival and presentation of local forms of performing arts: music, dance, drama and others. It runs a school for the training, teaching and documenting of Bhavai, Gujarat's local drama form. The school brings old masters, teachers and performers from the communities and provides them with financial support; it also awards scholarships to students. The Department also commissions research into local cultural practices and funds monographs on the same subject. It is in the process of setting up a museum to display the traditional costumes of Bhavai.

Responding to a renewed interest in using the performing arts to accelerate development, the Darpana Academy is offering its services in the field of development support communication. Darpana for Development is a unit that brings together the creative potential of its staff members and students to create modules of entertainment based on environmental issues, gender issues, adult education, hygiene, health care, communalism, corruption, modern farming techniques and other themes. Traditional combinations of skills are rediscovered in creative new formats. Through dance, drama and puppetry, the issues of untouchability, the exploitation of the poor and underprivileged, and the misuse of religious customs and traditions are depicted, criticised and discussed.[73]

Ganzeboom (1996: 154–5) confirms this, making it clear that there is a close association between education, arts training and cultural participation in later life. His research shows that art consumers are often more highly educated and have more often received arts training in school when compared with non-arts consumers. It would be naïve, Ganzeboom continues, to interpret these correlations as a simple causal chain, implying that art consumers are found to be highly educated. A slightly different conclusion is possible: art consumers have enjoyed a higher education, thanks to the encouraging home environment.

One popularising strategy employed by art institutions is to make art and culture more accessible to the general public. Some favoured tactics to make people 'culturally literate' are by: (1) making exhibitions more and more interactive, offering the public options in gathering information; (2) popularising the formats in setting up exhibitions; (3) introducing 'living history' by acting out historical events; and (4) introducing devices based on the new electronic media to enhance exhibitions. Conversely, a strategy for bringing popular culture (such as television soaps) closer to art appreciation is the introduction of media education into secondary education curriculum. Daily experience of the communication and information environment confronts young adults with art and design in a casual lived way. Media education is the development of competency in reading ubiquitous media messages critically.

Educational levels

Arts education within the basic education curriculum serves as a form of 'discovery learning'. It enables children to undertake a step-by-step discovery of various ways of thinking and thus to acquaint themselves with a more associative approach in ordering their social and physical environment.

A side-effect of including visual and performing arts in the basic educational curriculum is that it might strengthen the cultural (ethnic) and/or national identity. In countries making a huge effort to consolidate national identity (Papua New Guinea, for example) emphasis in art education is laid upon common traits among the aesthetic traditions of many disparate ethnic groups (in Papua New Guinea, more than seven hundred).

In the North Atlantic world, with its growing awareness of being a *multicultural society*, emphasis is placed on developing a tolerant attitude among children towards differences in experiencing the arts. 'At the same time, school curricula, which at the moment teach mostly the high arts, should include more teaching about popular and non-European arts' (Watanabe, 1996: 154–5).

In this context, music seems to appeal to children. It forms an integrated part of culture with which children become acquainted when very young. Developing different rhythms is one of the first things a child learns. Only at the age of six or seven will a distinctive experience of various melodies become explicit, corresponding to the age of entry into the basic education system. At that moment a child is very flexible in learning how to discriminate and appreciate rhythmic

Box 11.3 Papua New Guinea: art education policy after independence

Papua New Guinea became an independent nation in 1975. At the beginning of the 1980s, this country had an outspoken cultural policy, as reflected in the state budget. The former Prime Minister of Papua New Guinea, Michael Somare, showed a clear vision on this matter.[74] In a country with as many as 717 different ethnic groups, culture and art education are to be seen as contributing to national identity. Part of this policy was to set up a consistent, nationwide art education system.

The Expressive Arts curriculum takes the Papua New Guinean culture as its point of departure. This art education curriculum consists of several subjects which in other countries might be taught separately – such as drawing and painting, manual skills and music. The Expressive Arts curriculum has been designed by the National Education Board to create a more flexible educational approach towards the arts. This was based on the fact that in the traditional Melanesian society there is no real separation between the manufacturer of a drum and the musician who plays it, between the carver of a wooden mask and the person wearing it, between the costume maker and the dancer, between the composer and the singer.

To create qualified teachers in this area there was a need for art education at the tertiary level. In 1975 the National Arts School was called into being in Port Moresby. It was the first Pacific artistic training centre at the level of higher education. In a country where traditional wooden works of art and contemporary art might both be made by one and the same woodcarver, most of the people undergoing education still have one foot in the past and one in the future (Thompson, 1989: 48–9). For that reason traditional and contemporary artistic evolution are both subject to the same ongoing process.

and melodic cultural differences, especially when related to singing and movement.

In recent decades, according to Weitz (1988: 48), art education in general has been recognised as a means of strengthening the affinity of the art consumer for the various forms in which art manifests itself, teaching him or her to be a skilled reader, viewer, or listener, to deal critically with exposure to the work of art.

Especially in the South, where formal art education is still modest and considered a luxury, there are notable linkages to local and indigenous performing arts. South Asian and Indonesian training centres linked to higher education institutes (colleges and universities) have shown an ongoing interest in the 'living arts' within society at a local level, through the regular school system or out-of-school activities.

In fact, support of teacher training is considered a feedback mechanism which higher educational institutes employ in order to link up with basic education. An example is an environmental project started by the Darpana Academy, whose work is described in Boxes 3.2 11.2. The Academy, teachers and students at a basic educational level all worked together in order to make the students and other community members aware of the environmental issues at stake.

The distinction between the creative and appreciative components of art education, discussed above, is related to emphasis in the curriculum at different levels of formal education. The practical and creative component forms part of the art education curriculum at primary and secondary school levels. Practical skills training in art techniques such as drawing, painting, sculpture, music, drama and dance are not meant to turn students into artists but to introduce artistic skills to them.

Within the context of basic education, the main emphasis has been placed on active learning of skills. Skills training in the arts is not done through reading textbooks, but through practical exercises: learning by means of doing. The process of refining and controlling begins with their introduction to elementary practical skills in music, theatre, dance, art in general and literary expression (Tohmé, 1992: 21). Most often they learn through social experience: exposure to art processing situations and participation are more important than formal teaching. Children start to enjoy working on their own and in groups.

Within the context of advanced and secondary education the reflective way of studying the arts is introduced and integrated by providing historical and cultural information (such as knowledge of art and its history). Through participating in arts programmes at school, young adults come to value the arts and look forward to continued involvement with them. Showing a capacity for enjoyment and personal satisfaction as well as for making informed choices and judgments about the arts, the students at this level are confronted with the fact that 'art, as a presentational language of the senses, transmits meanings that cannot be transmitted through any other kind of language, such as discursive and *scientific* languages' (Bastos Barbosa, 1992: 3).

At a tertiary level the acquisition of artistic skills and reflection on the art(s) culminate in professional education in the arts or in the fine arts within the Faculty of the Arts at a university or other specialised higher educational institute, such as a School of Arts aiming at:

1 creation of a sound institutional basis on which to preserve the knowledge of art;

2 use of a proficient knowledge base to carry out research on art and publish its results;

3 acquisition of sufficient faculty members, quantitatively and qualitatively;

4 demonstration of high levels of creativity both intellectually (scripts, theses and dissertations) and practically in the form of art works;

5 cooperation with art groups within its sphere of influence to bring out their full potential; and

6 production of proficient graduates able to improve art education at elementary, secondary, and senior high school as well as higher education levels.

Box 11.4 Higher education in the arts in Indonesia

Indonesia declared independence in 1945, immediately after the end of the Second World War. During the 1970s and 1980s an art education policy and curriculum was developed by the Ministry of Education and Culture (MOEC) in Jakarta. With the application of new curricula for junior and senior high schools in 1975 and 1984, the need for higher education graduates to teach art subjects in the schools has increased. Recruitment of art teachers has been carried out through Diploma Programmes offered by teachers' training facilities in the universities together with professional art education offered by higher education institutes such as the Institute of Indonesian Arts (ISI) and the National College of Indonesian Arts (STSI).

The multi-stratified system of higher education called for in the Government Regulation of Indonesia demands programmes in arts as well as fine arts education at undergraduate, graduate and postgraduate levels to deliver both skilled and trained artists and scholars able to understand and improve knowledge of the arts by means of scientific studies.

In Indonesia (SPAFA, 1990) education in the arts at higher educational level is presented by the ISI (Yogjakarta), the STSI (Surakarta and Denpasar), the Indonesian Traditional Music Academy (ASKI)[75] in Padang Panjang, the National Academy of Indonesian Dance (ASTI)[76] in Bandung, the Jakarta Arts Institute (IKJ)[77] in Jakarta and several fine art and design study programmes at the Technology Institute of Bandung (ITB) and Udayana University (Bali). These are all art institutes offering education for various branches of art. Their programmes are planned so as to keep pace with the Indonesian multi-development programmes, particularly in science, technology and art, locally, nationally and internationally.

The STSI at Denpasar, mentioned above, falls under the authority of the Directorate General of Higher Education within the Ministry of Education and Culture. It was originally founded in 1967 by the regional government of Bali as the National Academy of Indonesian Dance (ASTI Denpasar), with the goal of training a new generation of artists and scholars to preserve, study and develop the performing arts. In 1969 the school became a national institute, an extension of ASTI Yogyakarta, under the authority of the Directorate General of Higher Education and Culture. Once placed directly under the Directorate General of Higher Education in 1976, it guided the establishment of the Institute of Indonesian Arts (ISI) together with other art academies in Indonesia.

After the founding of ISI Yogyakarta, which integrated the Academy of Indonesian Dance (ASTI), the Academy of Indonesian Music (AMI) and the Higher Institute of Indonesian Fine Arts (STSRI) in Yogyakarta, ASTI Denpasar was raised in status to become the College of Indonesian Arts (STSI Denpasar) in 1988. This Institute's learning process aims at the development of indigenous

Indonesian professionals sensitive to the needs of a diverse community as well as skillful and creative in their fields and dedicated to the nurturing of their national culture. The curriculum draws inspiration from the Five Principles (Pancasila) as stated in the 1945 Constitution, in addressing practical and theoretical subjects, including basic knowledge of the social sciences (anthropology) and the humanities (philosophy).

Teaching arts is as yet an incidental rather than than a structural part of education in most developing countries. The lack of trained personnel is a crucial problem. Of course, one does not need a specific curriculum to teach arts. All over the world enthusiastic and talented teachers in primary and secondary schools have become involved in art education. However, often there is no policy pressure to replace a teacher who has left the profession by one with similar talents in the arts field. More attention is paid to training qualified art teachers as part and parcel of (in-service) teacher training.

Another option to deal with a structural lack of art educators is to invite artists to visit schools and teach art. According to Avenstrup (1991: 56), local storytellers, dancers, carvers, basket-weavers, potters, textile workers, jewellers, musicians and singers are all artists whose knowledge and skills can be introduced into the classroom. They can actually help teach children the theory of arts and crafts as part of the process of passing on skills. Experiments have shown this during the 1970s in developing countries such as Papua New Guinea (see Box 11.3). It turned out that artists do indeed contribute to an increasing understanding of creative processes, developing artistic skills and building confidence with regard to the students' own creative abilities. The only requirements are remuneration and in-service training.

Opportunities

Worldwide, more and more attention is paid to arts education within the basic education curricula. This has been done for at least two reasons: to offer children a general cultural background and understanding of art in general, in theory as well as in practice; and to present children with the opportunity to discover their preferences and talents, preparing a number of them for future artistic education at a higher level.

One of the main problems within the cultural sector in developing countries is the lack of well-qualified manpower in arts and culture. The reasons for this are mainly cultural, political and economic. Islamic nations, for example, offer hardly any drama education at any educational level because their belief system does not allow living creatures (including human beings) to be represented in this way. Former communist or military regimes might have a strong tradition in performing arts (such as China or Myanmar) but are not charmed by TfD because its democratic principles are a precondition of this form of applied drama.

Central American and South and South-East Asian nations have fairly well-developed educational systems including curricula in art education at primary, secondary and tertiary levels. However, in many of these countries performing arts are still conceived either as traditional art forms to be preserved, or as mainstream art forms to be developed. In sub-Saharan Africa or Eastern Europe there are no economic resources available to start courses in arts management and administration or applied drama, and to train or upgrade people already working in the field. With the exception of a few visionaries there is not enough capacity at governmental or local level to organise 'culture and development' activities as a valuable part of cultural sectors.

This lack of educational infrastructure has never kept people from organising their own activities. The best-known examples are the Philippines, South Africa, India, Nigeria and a number of Central American states. In some of these countries networking began in order to improve the organisation of activities at a national level and to start collaborating with individuals, groups or even organisations in North America, the European Union or Australia. Due to these individual initiatives and the strong need for capacity building in the field of art and culture, several higher educational institutes in the North started MA courses in arts management and administration, applied drama or TfD in order to train people originating from developing or transitional countries. Few of these initiatives of the 1990s continued beyond the millennium. Preconditions are the availability of sufficient financial resources (grants, scholarships, bursaries) within the context of an adequate fellowship programme allowing students to attend a Euro-American higher educational institute, as well as the guarantee that the student will return to his or her home country after completing an education in the North.

Although, within the European context of international cooperation, bilateral fellowship programmes are offered in fields such as engineering, agriculture and economic planning, hardly any country offers bursaries to students wishing to be trained in the cultural sector – except for courses in heritage preservation, sustainable tourism and museum management. This lack of appropriate fellowship programmes is also the reason why few MA programmes set up in the North have succeeded over the years.

This leaves a few multilateral bursary programmes administered by organisations such as UNESCO. However, most of these grants are meant for students in the arts who have showed their excellence in one of the mainstream art forms or in the traditional art practices of their own countries. Few financial resources are available to train and upgrade 'culture and development' officials who might become cultural officers or 'trainers of trainers' in applied visual and performing arts at home. This is the reason why there is still a manpower deficiency in the cultural sector in developing countries and former Soviet states.

12
Conflicts and the Arts

What role can the arts play in conflict mediation and resolution?

Conflicts are universal

Conflict is a universal phenomenon occurring in all types of societies, in any country and between countries. The conflicts we are experiencing today have several causes. Most have to do with mistaken ownership. A common cause is 'landgrabbing'. For centuries migrants coming from outside occupied land belonging to the indigenous population. Yet another cause is exploitation of the natural and human resources by outsiders.

In many instances ethnic and/or religious differences tear countries apart. Sometimes the region's historical context and its geographical position exercise an influence, as recently illustrated in the Balkans and the Caucasus. In the Southern Philippines, parts of Indonesia (Atjeh, Timor, the Moluccan islands and Irian Jaya), Northern Ireland or Spain the main cause of conflicts between governments and the national liberation fronts or parties is of an ideological as well as a political nature.

In nations where a high degree of political oppression is exerted over certain regions, political parties or cultural minorities (examples include China, Myanmar and the Russian Federation), the current and still predominant attitude among those targeted has been one of active or passive resistance. The political expertise of interest groups leading political resistance in these countries has little chance to engage in cooperation with representatives of the ruling government.

Although officially national governments would like to see these 'rebellious' territories develop along mainstream lines, there is no actual desire to offer special opportunities to people and regions under oppressive government control. In such a situation the position of local officials is very ambivalent as regards who can work with whom, and for which purpose.

From pre- to post-independence

Nations have become independent in various ways. Those that experienced colonisation by a foreign oppressor may have opted for passive resilience, outspoken resistance or even a violent, armed fight for freedom.

After independence the nation is challenged to restore a balance between opposing groups. Building the country involves basic interventions such as preparing leaders for government responsibilities and free elections, political and economic reforms, setting up governmental institutions, writing a constitution, initiating rehabilitation programmes, and energising the infrastructure and national systems such as transport, health care, agriculture, community development, basic education and culture.

In order to succeed during the post-independence period it is imperative for the former liberation movement to ensure a full awareness of the new situation and of the implications (responsibilities and duties) of the peace agreements struck among the parties involved.

Self-determination is central to any progress towards reconciliation. However, in regions previously dominated by fear and oppression, self-determination is difficult to achieve. One of the first problems confronting newly formed governments in post-conflict situations is to replace the climate of fear and distrust with a sense of social cohesion. In general, this is done by articulating and working towards the goals of establishing equal rights and social justice for each and every citizen. Arts may play an important role during this process in terms of conflict prevention and intervention.

An important first step has been the building of an educational infrastructure in order (1) to educate the next generation by way of formal basic education; (2) to provide practical skills training by way of adult education; and (3) to offer opportunities to re-educate 'freedom fighters' for more civilian jobs. The next step is the introduction of long-term sector plans and national development plans, paying attention to Human Resource Development (HRD) programmes in order to help develop countries in a sustainable and long-term perspective.

In recent applications of TfD for political ends two extremes can be observed. It is either used in massive, large-scale national campaigns by the leading government or political party in power, or opposing parties apply it on a very small-scale. In both cases, TfD touches upon a difference or even a conflict of interests.

However, in situations in which theatre injects information in support of political lobbying, propagating ideas that may lead to reforms within the community or the society at large, the emphasis lies much more on the application of theatre as a product. Here stage performances characterised by dramatic rhetoric appeal to the public.

In Namibia, colonial rule ceased after an armed and violent struggle for freedom led by the South West African People's Organisation (SWAPO). Neighbouring South Africa – colonial trustee under a UN mandate following a history of German colonisation – treated Namibia as a fifth province, applying its apartheid laws and 'Bantu Education' system.

Box 12.1 Using music training for traumatised war children in Cambodia

'Culture is the soul of our people. Without a soul, without art our people cannot exist,' says Proeung Chhieng, director of the dance department of the School of Fine Arts in Phnom Penh (Cambodia) in an interview with van Veghel (1990: 10). Although the people of Cambodia have not enjoyed peace for more than twenty years, this conservatoire in its capital is a home to some 600 students in dance, music and visual arts.

In earlier times, the patronage of Cambodian artists lay in the hands of the aristocracy, the monasteries and the landed gentry. However, with the coming of Pol Pot not only were most of the Cambodian nobility killed, but so were their functionaries and *protégés*, such as artists. Thousands were arrested, kept in camps, tortured and murdered. Costumes and instruments were destroyed, as well as scripts, books and performance scores.

For that reason, at the conservatoire in Phnom Penh traditional dances and pieces of music are literally being 'restored'. The few old artists who survived the Khmer Rouge violence, without any written references or visual documentation, are trying to recollect performing scores and transfer them to younger generations of performing artists.

Most of the dance pieces, however, are irretrievably lost. Of more than twenty dances in the repertory, explains Proeung Chhieng, the women have only been able fully to reconstruct three, and only an hour or two of many five-act ballets that traditionally started at 7 pm and lasted until dawn (Blaustein, 1989: 44).

NGOs, too, are involved in giving arts education a new start. The Music School Kampot[78] forms part of the Khmer Cultural Development Institute, a Cambodian non-governmental organisation. This music school is unique for Cambodia, stimulating and promoting the preservation and re-establishment of traditional music.

The school provides an opportunity for today's children to be trained in these time-honoured cultural expressions. Its targeted audience consists of children with a war trauma, orphans and abused or handicapped children. Apart from those severely wounded and mutilated by landmines, children are physically affected for life by neglecting diseases like polio. Music and dance may be of help to them in coping with their past.

The school houses about thirty children aged four to eighteen. In the morning they are trained by Maes Saem, a music teacher related to the Royal Palace. The children play on instruments which are replicas of authentic instruments destroyed by the Pol Pot regime. Physically able children participate in dance classes in order to learn the traditional Khmer dances. In the afternoon they attend a more regular class programme.

The school orchestra performs during concerts and public ceremonies, providing extra fund-raising opportunities for the school. This orchestra has toured Europe several times. A compact disc has been produced presenting its repertory.

A certain relationship exists between the school and the National Theatre whereby very talented students are offered an opportunity to perform with the National Theatre in due course. By stimulating this warm relationship between the local school and the national theatre environment it is hoped that, through the arts, a better understanding of disabled and physically handicapped people will grow within Cambodian society in the long run.

In Namibia's colonial past the educational system and its close power alliance with the missionary religion had caused a systematic cultural disinheritance. Art subjects in schools and other educational institutions were taught in accordance to the classical Anglo-German culture. Not only white students, but also a curriculum based on white traditions in the performing arts dominated the higher educational system, including the university's drama department.

Prior to Namibia's independence there were two distinct phenomena: community theatre spread over the rural areas and theatre largely meant for white urban audiences. The national playhouse in Windhoek, the National Theatre of Namibia (NTN), was mainly used for concerts and had little connection with the communities in the countryside. Community theatre was a powerful if sometimes unsophisticated means of expression, without a strong organisation as expressed in the urban setting by Bricks, The Windhoek Players, Playmakers and some youth theatre. However, there were many activities, both within and in addition to churches, trade unions and cultural groups, directly voicing Namibian needs and situations.

Independence brought with it a new dimension to all these cultural activities. The Ministry of Education and Culture developed a nationwide Arts Education and Training Programme. It advanced a reconciliation in national artistic capacity building within the Namibian visual and performing arts. A preliminary reform of the curriculum for junior secondary education offered drama, dance, art and music as optional subjects, and arts appreciation as an obligatory course for all. Schools were invited to initiate projects in identifying and celebrating local culture and artists, as well as finding suitable materials from the oral tradition to be included in school curricula, arts, language and literature programmes.

The Arts and Culture Directorate of the Ministry took care of general cultural promotion at various levels. However, at the society's grassroots level part of the work was done by cultural officers in the various districts and regions, stimulating the set-up of cultural clubs in rural areas far away from Windhoek. Some clubs included music and dance activities as well as the initiation of museums, libraries, craft activities and sport clubs at local level.

Namibia's situation at independence was quite different from that confronting peoples who have fought successfully for self-government in a non-violent way, such as the Inuit people of Northern Canada.[79] In their fight for autonomy the latter were more involved in legal than in military strategies. As a result the Inuit had an opportunity to develop policy structures, legal bodies and long-term development plans along the way to obtaining self-government.

In a post-conflict situation necessary measures need to be taken in order to reconcile factions within the population. The young generation must be taught to look forward and not to fall back on the ways of resistance ingrained in the lives of their parents. Policies must be developed and implemented in order to guarantee personal security and individual rights. The country has to be rebuilt in terms of infrastructure and human resource development.

In addition, serious socio-economic underdevelopment and lack of a local cadre need to be addressed. Providing basic education is an important prerequisite. Medical measures, influencing demographic developments, are important stabilising factors. The people themselves need to build a local infrastructure for this to be effectively implemented in order to influence their future. Educating individuals to take up positions in local government is a basic condition for improving living standards and social development.

National reconciliation dictates that cultural development, like all other development at national level, must make existing infrastructure relevant to the needs of the people.

A systemic view

In Table 12.1 an attempt has been made to systematise the role the arts play, showing its most important opportunities to provide support in the struggle for a better society before and after reaching independence, as well as the implications for the individual, the community and society at large. There is a striking congruence between the support offered by using the arts and the general principles of conflict management.

In pre-independence the role of the arts focuses on motivation, encouragement, inspiration and organisation. After independence the arts place more emphasis on understanding, dialogue, conflict resolution and cohesion.

To conclude this chapter, Figure 12.1 presents the main functions of the visual and performing arts in (potential) situations of conflict. Examples demonstrating the figure's four quadrants might be the following:

• Applying *visual arts* in terms of a *process*-oriented approach as in *community building* with ghetto children in Washington by means of painting a mural opposing hand-gun violence;
• Applying the arts in terms of a *product*-oriented approach to reconciliation as in the *performance* of the South African anthem or in the performance of *Romeo and Juliet* in the West Bank;
• Applying the *performing arts* in terms of a *process*-oriented approach as in music education as part of the *therapeutic rehabilitation* offered to war-traumatised children in Cambodia (see Box 12.1);
• Applying the *visual arts* in terms of a *product*-approach as in the installation of *memorial* monuments and *commemorative* works of art.

Table 12.1 Applications of the arts in the struggle for a better society: pre- and post-independence

Level	Role of the arts	
	Pre-independence	**Post-independence**
Society	Experiment with alternative visions of future society; Develop alternative and playful visions which outline the envisaged nation and its organisation; Support the planning for alternative strategies to build up the nation as envisaged; Mediate between parties involved, especially beyond the medium of the spoken dialogue; Encourage the various (conflicting) parties involved not to close the door to an ongoing dialogue; Train (by means of simulation) people to gain control over their participation in political and socio-economic systems.	Stimulate processes of democratisation and rehabilitation (e.g., drama performances to stimulate voter behaviour); Increase understanding and appreciation of divergent world views; Articulate and work towards achieving equal rights and social justice (gender- and ethnic-specific items); Integrate art education within the national curriculum as a means to reconciliation and peace education for the next generation; Facilitate continuing dialogues at important moments in the process of intercession and mediation.
Community	Inspire new visions based on trust and faith; Reach a working consensus within the community on fundamental issues; Create a sound organisational basis at local level; Develop strategies for future community leaders.	Contribute to community development and community organisation; Improve community interaction and socialisation; Support in dismantling a climate of fear and distrust; Contribute to creating cultural cohesion; Use the arts to educate and train the adult population (including collaborators, former freedom fighters, refugees in exile and community dwellers); Make people aware not only of their rights but also of their responsibilities.

Table 12.1 cont.

| Level | Role of the arts | |
	Pre-independence	Post-independence
Individual	Prepare the people for independence; Contribute to identity building; End ethnic stereotyping.	Contribute to conflict resolution; Empower ethnic groups; Address cognitive, affective and social needs; Negotiate peace and strive for reconciliation; Teach mutual respect and understanding; Support personal security and individual rights; Take away ethnic stereotyping; Support therapeutic treatment of post-war traumatised adults and children.

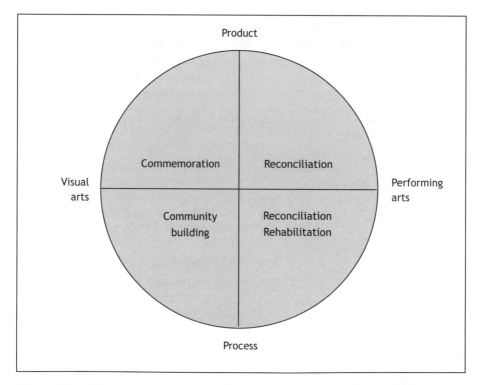

Figure 12.1 The arts and their main functions in creating a just society

Appendices

Appendix 1. Videos on TfD

Title	*ACTPA African Centre for the Training of Performing Arts, at Castle Arts, Bulawayo, Zimbabwe, 1990*
Creator	
Production	
Distribution	African Theatre Exchange (ATEX)
Year	1990
Duration	*c.*15 minutes
System	VHS/PAL
Language	English
Detail	Colour; mediocre quality images
Entry	Zimbabwe; culture and development; theatre; training.

In 1990 the African Theatre Exchange (ATEX) launched the ACPTA (African Centre for the Training of Performing Arts), a project set up with financial aid from the government of Zimbabwe and SIDA, NORAD, DANIDA and UNESCO. In November of that year the first training exercise began in Castle Arts, Bulawayo: a nine-week course dealing with 'dance drama in contemporary Africa', open to theatre producers from all over Africa and aimed at the exchange of experiences, specific expressions of drama and methods.

The video introduces ACTPA's goals, reports on the above course as well as on the official inauguration of the training centre in Bulawayo. Footage from the dance drama *Footprints* follows.

Title	*Stringing out for a Change*
Creator	Anamaria Decock
Production	IEC Project UNFPA/FAO Burundi
Distribution	Information Division, FAO, Rome

137

Year	1990
Duration	24 minutes
System	VHS/PAL
Language	English
Details	Colour; English commentary
Entry	Burundi; population education; family planning; health education; puppet theatre.

Popular forms of culture (theatre, dance, music) are succesfully applied as empowerment and training instruments. These expressions combine tuition and amusement and can attract large groups. The shows, generally speaking, serve to confront the public with its problems in the hope of a constructive discussion afterwards. This may mark the start of a combined effort to deal with the problems at hand.

The film reports on the use of puppet theatre in support of population education activities in Burundi, dealing with the process of testing puppets and the shows in which polygamy and birth control, in relation to welfare issues, are discussed. Afterwards discussions with the public take place.

Title	*Theatre for Development, the Kanyama Theatre Group*
Creator	Darlington Chongo
Production	Lima Time, ZBC
Distribution	Werner Haas Video Productions
Year	1991
Duration	25 minutes
System	VHS/PAL
Language	English
Details	Colour; English sub-titles; an episode of Lima Time, an agricultural educational programme produced by Zambia television.
Entry	Zambia; theatre for development; education; empowerment.

Popular forms of culture (theatre, dance, music) are succesfully applied as empowerment and training instruments. These expressions combine learning and amusement and can attract large groups. The shows, generally speaking, serve to confront the public with its problems in the hope of a constructive discussion afterwards. This may mark the start of a combined effort to deal with the problems at hand.

This film reports on the use of drama in order to support developmental activities in Zambia. The Kanyama Theatre Group's working process in creating a show consists of (1) an inventory of the problems existing within the society (through interviews with villagers); (2) an analysis of assessed problems; (3) setting the show up and elaborating it; and (4) the actual event in the village. Afterwards the public is divided into small groups in order to discuss the show's contents.

Title   *Puppets against AIDS*
Creator   Harriet Gavshon
Production   Gary Friedman
Distribution   African Research and Educational Puppetry Programme
Year   1991
Duration   8 minutes
System   VHS/PAL
Language   English
Details   Colour
Entry   South Africa; puppet theatre; education; AIDS

Popular forms of culture (theatre, dance, music) are successfully applied as empowerment and training instruments. These expressions combine learning and amusement and can attract large groups. The shows, generally speaking, serve to confront the public with its problems in the hope of a constructive discussion afterwards. This may mark the start of a combined effort to deal with the problems at hand.

The film reports on the activities of the African Research and Educational Puppetry Programme (AREPP) as founded in Southern Africa (1987). The AREPP offers education on AIDS by means of shows with life-size puppets. The puppeteers are health workers. Comics (with the same message) and condoms are distributed after the shows. The footage includes fragments of shows, both in the city and the countryside, in front of the armed forces and at school.

Title   *Creative Path/Phillipine Educational Theatre Association*
Creator   Soxy Topiaco
Production   BUGKOS
Distribution
Year   1991
Duration   10 minutes/60 minutes
System   VHS/PAL
Language   English
Details   Colour
Entry   Philippines; culture; empowerment; educational theatre.

Applying art and culture (including theatre) in processes of development and political empowerment.

Creative Path is a short documentary in which the coming into existence and the aims of BUGKOS are explained. BUGKOS supervises some 340 cultural organisations in the Philippines. Its mission is to stimulate the population's artistic skills and to apply art to the benefit of the population's social and political emancipation.

Creative Path is followed by a series of registrations of theatre shows and workshops of PETA, the Philippine Educational Theatre Association. They serve empowerment and social action. PETA organises theatre workshops for various social groups.

Title	*Development Theatre: a Way to Listen*
Creator	Alex Mavrocordatos and Bianivo Munkoro
Production	SOS Sahel Drama Unit
Distribution	SOS Sahel, London, UK
Year	
Duration	13 minutes
System	VHS/PAL
Language	English
Details	Colour; videotaped slide show
Entry	Mali; empowerment; participation; forms of traditional dance and drama.

Popular forms of culture (theatre, dance, music) are successfully applied as empowerment and training instruments. These expressions combine learning and amusement and can attract large groups. The shows, generally speaking, serve to confront the public with its problems in the hope of a constructive discussion afterwards. This may mark the start of a combined effort to deal with the problems at hand.

The film deals with traditional dance and drama forms on an SOS Sahel project amongst the Bobo people of Mali. In this project the villagers themselves perform, not the outsiders, creating a show based on their perception of a problem and thereby confronting project workers and government staff.

Title:	*The Tale of Two Latrines: Water Woes*
Director:	Loukie Levert
Producer:	BKH Consulting Engineers/Programme Advisory Team (PAT)
Year:	1994
Length:	10 minutes
Language:	English
System:	VHS
Details:	Colour
Keywords:	Kenya; Theatre for Development; sanitation; hygiene; preventive health care; pit latrines

This video is a visual aid used in the training of project teams within the Rural Domestic Water Supply and Sanitation Programme II (RDWSSP), as implemented in the Nyanza Province (Kenya) through the Lake Basin Development Authority, on the instigation of the Ministry of Land Reclamation and with the assistance of the Kenyan and Netherlands governments. The Programme Advisory Team (PAT) of BKH consultants (Kisumu/Delft/Nairobi) were involved in the practical implementation of the projects. The objectives of this programme focus on providing: (1) safe and accessible water, (2) safe and low-cost disposal of human waste, ensuring user participation and responsibility for facilities. The video is based on a pilot project on TfD for Water and Sanitation Messages.

The Tale of Two Latrines presents us with three very brief sketches, without any dialogue. The storyline relates to the happiness a newly constructed latrine 'experiences' after being cleaned by each user. Another latrine located just outside the village is less happy. It feels sad, lonely and neglected – attracting no users at all because it is filthy and unhygienic. The accompanying slapstick music – as in silent-movies – emphasises the story and the acting. Comments are given by means of text blocks between scenes.

This video recording is meant to present specialists and experts with an impression of how TfD has been used during the implementation phase of this project. In particular it deals with the way in which the themes of workshops are transcribed into storylines and performances.

Title:	*Participatory Methods Used in RDWSSP Participation in Practice*
Director:	Loukie Levert[80]
Producer:	BKH Consulting Engineers/Programme Advisory Team (PAT)
Year:	1995
Length:	20 minutes
Language:	English
System:	VHS
Details:	Colour
Keywords:	Kenya; Theatre for Development; sanitation; hygiene; preventive health care; pit latrines

One of the objectives of the RDWSSP-II project (see above) was to make the local community aware of the relationship between hygiene and the spread of diseases. During its implementation phase the project sought to inform the local community – by means of theatre and theatre games – about sanitary behaviour, such as the use and cleaning of latrines and the washing of hands in order to prevent contamination with bacteria.

In 1995 Loukie Levert, who was involved in this project as a 'development support communication' expert, produced and directed a series of four short instructive videos on the use of TfD within the context of sanitation projects. Initially the tapes were made to present development experts and representatives of the donor organisations with a better insight into the use and effectiveness of the TfD approach, by rendering a step-by-step impression of the use of this medium as a development support communication device. Later on the staff explored the instructive value of these videos.

The videos, ranging from ten to twenty minute tapes, start with a very general overview of the very specific use of TfD in this context. The first tape is a documentary case study on Kanyadiro, the project's location, and shows the general context of the RDWSSP-II. This video is a visual aid on the training of project teams and staff members within the RDWSSP.

Title:	*Theatre for Development: a Pilot Project*
Director:	Loukie Levert
Producer:	BKH Consulting Engineers/Programme Advisory Team (PAT)
Year:	1995
Length:	15 minutes
Language:	English
Particularities:	Colour
System:	VHS
Keywords:	Kenya; theatre for development; sanitation; hygiene; preventive health care; pit-latrines

This video is a visual aid to the training of project teams within the RDWSSP-II (see above), and is based on a pilot project on TfD for Water and Sanitation Messages.

By reviewing a step-by-step project cycle in the use of TfD, the video introduces the project's aims. Next, it explains how the various theatre disciplines (song, dance, music, dialogue and pantomime) are applied within the project's context. It shows how the actors make an effort to deal with the audience in an interactive manner. Brief sketches bring out the moments in which members of the audience have a choice to react towards correct and incorrect hygienic behaviour. The dialogue and sketches are full of humour. The male actors play female characters. This brief documentary ends with a summary of steps and results in the application of TfD to this specific project.

Title:	*Community Theatre: Global Perspectives*
Year:	May 2003
Producer:	Memphis Film and Television/Stichting Ocean Film Productions (Utrecht)
Length:	91 minutes
Video systems:	Available on VHS-PAL and VHS-NTSC
Director:	Rod Prosser
Executive	Producer: Eugene van Erven (Ocean Film Productions)
Distributor:	Routledge (www.Routledge.com, or 11, New Fetter Lane, London (EC4P 4EE UK or at Routledge USA: 29 West 35th Street, New York NY 10001)

Community Theatre is an important device enabling communities to share their stories, participate in dialogue, and break down the increasing exclusion of marginalised groups. It is practised all over the world by growing numbers. Eugene van Erven, an expert on political theatre and author of *Radical People's Theatre*

(1988) and *The Playful Revolution: Theatre and Liberation in Asia* (1992) has put together the first comparative study concerning the work and methodological traditions as developed in community theatres around the world. This broad research is based on van Erven's experiences with community theatre groups in six very different countries. Together with a unique video record of van Erven's journey, specially produced to accompany the book, *Community Theatre* provides us with:

1   a sociological impression of Marinduque (the Philippines), Utrecht (the Netherlands), Los Angeles (USA), Puntarenas (Costa Rica), Sigoti (Kenya) and Western Sydney (Australia);
2   a brief history of the local community theatre;
3   a guide to the local arts scene;
4   a background to the featured artists;
5   a case study of a specific community theatre project.

The video has the same title as the accompanying paperback (Routledge, 2001).[81] It is divided into brief 15-minute documentaries that parallel the book's contents. The documentaries have a common framework, following the creative origins of each group as local community theatre from the first meeting to the opening night of the first public performance.

Appendix 2. Project Cycle Management (PCM) and research instruments

Table A2.1 Project Cycle Management (PCM) and related research instruments

Phase	Definition	Research activities
1 Indicative programming	Establishing general guidelines and principles for donor cooperation, this phase covers the sectional and thematic focusing of support/assistance in a country or region and may set out ideas for projects/ programmes.	*Diagnostic studies* done prior to the implementation phase, basically in order to describe, explain and predict what will happen with and without the project.
2 Identification	Initial formulation of project ideas in terms of objectives, results and activities aimed at establishing whether or not it is worth going ahead with a feasibility study. Another instrument is the stakeholder analysis, fashionable during the early 1990s, particularly among Northern NGOs adopting the strategic planning model. A stakeholder analysis attempts to identify the nature of the interests of the stakeholders involved; to suggest how they can contribute to the initiative; and to highlight potential conflicts. This analysis may indicate whether the interests of the stakeholders are compatible, and if there is a need to negotiate on competing expectations and priorities (Eade, 1997: 125).	*Feasibility study:* studying the project's effectiveness and efficiency which in the long run will be 'translated' into the sustainability of the project activities. *Stakeholder analysis:* a methodology aiming to define the actors with 'stakes' or interests in a development programme. All kinds of stakeholders can be included in the analysis: individuals and organisations, those directly connected to the programme and those whose connections are more indirect. A stakeholder analysis tries to identify the nature of everyone's interests; what they can contribute to the initiative and which potential conflicts we should be prepared for (Seppälä, 2000:36).

3 Appraisal/ formulation	All the project's details are specified on the basis of a feasibility study. It is of considerable importance that decision makers and those planning and carrying out the projects/programmes play an active part in the preliminary phase, i.e. the identification stage.	*Internal examination* of the project's merits and the way it fits in with sectoral policies. This leads to a decision on whether or not to draw up a financing proposal.
4 Financing	Drafting of the financing proposal, presenting the estimated costs per activity and parts thereof per calendar year for the entire duration of the project.	*The budget* is the workplan's financial 'translation'. After the proposal has been examined decisions are taken on its approval. This is followed by the drafting and signing of a financing agreement which provides for several implementation phases; the start of the following stage will normally depend on the conclusions reached after evaluating the previous stage.
5 Implementa- tion	Actual execution of the project's action plan by drawing on the resources provided for in the financing agreement in order to achieve the desired results and the project's purpose: the drafting of plan of operation and the monitoring of reports. Research instruments applied in this phase are, among others, monitoring, SWOT analysis, rapid evaluations and needs assessments. Before a project actually starts a SWOT analysis (Strengths, Weaknesses, Opportunities and Threats) is recommended.	*Monitoring* is an instrument which allows management to adequately follow the implementation of a project. Monitoring is the process of collecting and analysing information on a regular basis for the purpose of checking on progress in project implementation. This should allow the project management to adjust activities, inputs and budgets where necessary in order to realise the aims on which the project is based. *SWOT analysis:* aims at identifying any weaknesses and strengths in the implementation process in order to maximise

Strengths have been built up in the past and are provided for by the context/environment; weaknesses are insufficiently developed qualities; while opportunities are the strong qualities, effectively organised for the future.

First, a SWOT analysis retrospectively identifies and analyses a project/programme's or sector's strong and weak qualities; it then organises its strong qualities into future opportunities without neglecting weaknesses from the past as potential threats for the future.

efficiency and to make optimal use of resources and facilities. *Rapid evaluations:* joint identification, along with the local population, of elements likely to favour or hinder a development project. This instrument is somewhere between participatory research and evaluation studies, conducted for and/or by development practitioners in order to require information on an urgent basis as part of the monitoring process. In the rural context so-called Rapid Rural Appraisals (RRAs) are used. *Needs assessment* is a continuing process of needs analysis as part of monitoring a project/ programme, including an ongoing reflection on 'what happens' within and outside the programme, and to its actors involved in a process of sharing as part of their ongoing partner-ship. In order to meet the needs of these actors, a needs-assessment has to be imple-mented in close collaboration with the primary and other stakeholders in the community.

---

6 Evaluation

Evaluation is a process attempting to determine as systematically and objectively as possible the relevance, effectiveness and impact of activities (during or after implementation) in the light of their objectives. Evaluation is undertaken with a view to possible remedial action and/or framing of recommendations for

Final evaluations are external (mostly not conducted by persons affiliated with executing organisations).[82] They tend to be carried out bureaucratically to meet a certain requirement:
1 to determine the effectiveness of development activities after completion;
2 to collect data on the achieve-ments of the participants/

the guidance of similar future projects. Because evaluations are conducted before, during and after the project's completion there are different classes/types of evaluation: diagnostic studies, assessments and follow-up studies.

For diagnostic studies, see step 1 of this table.

stakeholders;

3 to assess the activity's effects and to improve future development activities;

4 to grade the participants' achievement, providing information on how primary stakeholders have changed with respect to the aims of development activities.

Assessments made upon the project's completion in order to ascertain whether its objectives were fulfilled, and to learn from experience so as to improve the process of future project planning.

Impact evaluation asks the question: did the impact result from the project measures? In other words, is it possible to establish a cause–effect relation? Final impact: have its objectives been reached? Has the programme achieved what it set out to do? For programme donors this is the most important question to answer.

Follow-up studies are conducted after a certain lapse of time in order to determine if the impact corresponds to the projected goals, and if any unanticipated consequences have occurred (regarding the environment, focus group, or organisation implementing the project).

Appendix 3. MA courses in the UK

University of Warwick

The Centre for Cultural Policy Studies offers opportunities for the postgraduate study of arts management; cultural policy in Europe (including the UK); and the creative and media industries.

The Centre's distinctive approach is its engagement with both the practical realities of working in the cultural sector and with theoretical questions around the conditions of contemporary culture. The Centre is thus particularly attractive to students wishing to develop their careers and at the same time reflect on the wider implications of their work within a stimulating intellectual environment.

The Centre offers three taught MA courses: the MA in European Cultural Policy and Management (established in 1992); the MA in Creative and Media Enterprises (established in 1999) and the MA in International Design and Communication (established in 2005). Students may also register for research degrees, leading to the award of MA, MPhil or PhD in Cultural Policy Studies.

The Centre for Cultural Policy Studies and the School of Theatre, Performance and Cultural Policy Studies collaborate in research work leading to the degrees of MA, MPhil and PhD in Theatre Studies. In Theatre Studies, suitably qualified candidates may now offer practice-based work as a component of a PhD. Current research interests are 'Theatre-Historical Research into Performance, Text and Architecture' and 'Contemporary Theatre and Performance'. (http://www2.warwick.ac.uk/ study/postgraduate/arts/cultural/)

University of Manchester, The School of Arts, Histories and Cultures [83]

Drama at Manchester's Masters programme in Applied Theatre is open to graduates who are interested in the application of theatre in social policy or educational fields. It offers both a research and practical opportunity to study theatre in a range of dynamic and challenging settings, from theatre in prisons to theatre in education. It offers students the chance to develop their own practical work and skills, and apply these to projects of their choice. Students have worked in a range of locations – from Strangeways Prison Manchester to factories in Peru. Students have researched creative work with special needs young people to theatre-based anger management courses. The course is proudly multidisciplinary, combining aspects of participatory theatre, criminology, psychology, education and social policy. From 2000–1, a new option has been available: in collaboration with The National Trust, a specialist pathway has been developed in the use of theatre and theatre techniques in the interpretation of heritage sites and museum collections. This is a growing area of applied theatre practice which will be studied through both seminar and practical, site-based experience.

Aims: To encourage the research of theatre and drama applied to non-traditional spaces and marginalised communities. To enable students to interrogate and evaluate their own and their peers' practice.

Objectives: That by the end of the course students will have participated in and analysed a theatre project in the criminal justice or educational system (including heritage education); initiated their own theatre-based project within a community of their choice; analysed and evaluated their own practice; developed academic strength in disciplines related to the field; accomplished a substantial piece of original research.

The programme structure is 1 year full-time registration or 2 year part-time.

(http://www.arts.manchester.ac.uk/subjectareas/drama/postgraduatestudy/ maappliedtheatre/)

University of Leeds, School of English[84]

The School of English offers a 12-month full-time programme on 'Theatre and Development Studies'. This MA programme is an interdisciplinary degree taught by staff from The Workshop Theatre and the Centre for Development Studies. The programme responds to a perceived need for, on the one hand, development personnel engaging with the arts to understand how to use creative processes within development and educational contexts, and on the other for arts practitioners working with development partners to understand the theories and methodologies behind development practice.

Students undertaking the course will have the opportunity to:
- Study a range of approaches to development strategy and theory
- Investigate the uses of theatre within education and development environments
- Make community-based theatre and take it into a community context
- Make links with development and community arts professionals
- Undertake individual study on a dissertation topic of their choice
- Choose from a range of theatre and development options in order to slant the MA in the particular direction that most interests them

Compulsory core modules:
- The Uses of Theatre
- Development Theories, Strategies and Issues
- Research Methodology for Development
- Research Methodologies and Bibliography
- Dissertation

Optional modules:
- African Theatre
- Documenting Theatre
- Traditional Chinese Theatre
- Gender and Development (Policy & Practice)
- Gender, Globalisation and Development
- Development Management Techniques
- Political Economy of Resources and Development
- Rural Development

For detailed information on the content of the modules see:
http://www.leeds.ac.uk/theatre/ma/ma2.html .

University of Wales, Aberystwyth
Department of Theatre, Film and Television Studies[85]

The department offers a taught Masters in Theatre and the World. In the programme, the phenomenon of theatre is approached in its worldwide cultural context(s). The phrase 'and the world' is doubly pertinent, since at the heart of the MA are two beliefs: firstly a commitment to international exploration; and secondly the tenet that theatre never exists as an isolated phenomenon, but as an integral part of the society – the 'world' – in which it has developed. The course is a broad and varied one, which includes seminar-based teaching, practical work, and independent research.

Some of the key features of the course include:

* Its attention to the international and intercultural dimensions of theatre and performance.
* Its balance of academic and practical methods of study.
* Its opportunities to encounter visiting practitioners and researchers from around the world.

For more information see: http://www.aber.ac.uk/tfts/en/teaching/schemes/postgrad/theatre/

The Department also offers opportunities for full-time or part-time study towards the MPhil and PhD degrees in a number of different areas including modern and contemporary Welsh, American, English and European drama, the social function of theatre and various aspects of film and television.

King Alfred's University College, University of Warwick

Box 5.1 in Chapter 5 provides information on the MA in Theatre and Media for Development.

For further information see http://www.winchester.ac.uk/?Page=3826 .

Appendix 4. Networking

Regional networks

The ministers of education and culture of the South-East Asian nations were the first to concentrate their powers to encourage research programmes at the tertiary level of the formal education system, including the arts. The South-East Asian Ministers of Education Organisation (SEAMEO) initiated a South-South research network called the SEAMEO Regional Centre for Archaeology and Fine Arts (SPAFA). This collaborative research programme into the arts and fine arts includes South–South cooperation in research projects in the fields of archaeology, maritime archaeology, fine arts and performing arts.

International networks

There is a definite need for international networks bringing together practitioners and theoreticians interested in art and art education beyond the Euro-American context in order to enlarge the expertise, skills and insight of artists, art educators and researchers from all over the world by means of promoting and supporting intercultural exchange and mutual cooperation.

The many international networks include: (1) Creative Exchange (the Network for Culture and Development) in London; (2) the Paris-based International Fund for the Promotion of Culture, an official UNESCO body; (3) Culture Link, the Network of Networks for Research and Cooperation in Cultural Development, sponsored by UNESCO; (4) the Council of Europe; (5) the British American Arts Association (BAAA); (6) the International Arts and Education Network; (7) the European Network of Art Organisations for Children and Young People (EUNETART); (8) the European League for Institutes of the Arts (ELIA); and (9 the International Amateur Theatre Association/ Organisation for Understanding and Education through Theatre (AITA/IATA).

Some international cultural networks are organised as non-governmental organisations (NGOs), recognised by UNESCO; among them are the International Theatre Institute, the International Music Council and the International Council of Museums.

Table A4.1 Cultural networks (not exhaustive)

		National	**Multilateral**
Individual(s)		Professional associations and labour unions: Guild of Nigerian Dancers (GOND), National Association of Nigerian Theatre Arts Practitioners (NANTAP), Association of Nigerian Authors (ANA), Society of Nigerian Theatre Artists (SONTA)	International Federation of Actors (IFA)
Institutional	NGOs	Nigerian Association for Oral History and Tradition (NAOHT); Zimbabwean Association of Community Theatre (ZACT); Kenya Drama/Theatre and Education Association (KDEA); Association for Native Development in the Performing and Visual Arts (ANDPVA); People's Educational Theatre (PET) association in Swaziland; Philippine Educational Theatre Association (PETA)	International Theatre Institute; International Music Council; International Council of Museums; International Amateur Theatre; Association-Organisation for Under-standing and Education through Theatre (AITA/IATA); Latin American Centre for Theatre Creation and Inves-tigation (CELCIT); Eastern Caribbean Popular Theatre Organisation (ECPTO)
	GOs	Japan Council of Performers' Organizations (Geidankyo)	SPAFA; EITALC, the International Association of Latin American and Caribbean Theatre Schools
Individual and Institutional		National Association for Drama in Education (NADIE)	IDEA; International Fund for the Promotion of Culture (UNESCO); Creative Rights Forum; Culture Link; International Arts and Education Network; the European Network of Art Organizations for Children

Table A4.1 cont.

National	Multilateral
	and Young People (EUNETART); European League for Institutes of the Arts (ELIA); British American Arts Association (BAAA); Informal European Theatre Meeting (IETM);[86] International Centre for Theatre in Education (ICTIE)

Notes

1   *Theatre in Search of Social Change* (1989) brought together various experiences in Theatre for Development (TfD) during the 1970s and 1980s, presenting examples from all over the world but mostly referring to efforts made in Nicaragua, Cuba, the Philippines, India and China to apply theatre within the context of adult education.

2   Ngugi wa Thiong'o (b. 1938) served a 12-month prison sentence in Kenya during the late 1970s after one of his plays was used as an organising tool to urge peasants to rebel against their exploitation. In 1982 he went into self-imposed exile in London.

3   Meanwhile Freire's ideas have been extensively criticised. For an interesting article in this context, see Alan Rogers, 1992.

4   'Conscientisation is a process in which the people try to understand their present situation in terms of the prevailing social, economic and political relationships in which they find themselves. This analysis of reality must be undertaken by the people who can decide what their important needs and experiences are, and not by experts'. (Burkey, 1993: 55)

5   See the website of the Royal Tropical Institute (KIT).

6   Teatro La Candelaria (founded in 1966) became important to the development of a new theatre movement (Movimiento del Nuevo Teatro) in Central American dramaturgy as Teatro Experimental de Cali (TEC) (Cali is a Colombian city), which began its work in 1958 under the dynamic direction of Enrique Buenaventura.

7   According to Musa (1998: 151), 'Two groups that have championed the cause of Theatre for Development in West Africa are the universities/colleges and non-governmental organizations.'

8   Readers may consult David Kerr's excellent essay on the early history of TfD in Southern Africa: see Kerr, 1999.

9   Lee Dale Byam has described this part of the contemporary history of TfD very well in 'Post-colonialism, Development, and a New African Theatre', Chapter 1 in Byam, 1999.

10 Ross Kidd met R. A. Leis when the latter was working at the Centre of Studies and Social Action (CEASPA), Panama.

11 Deutsche Stiftung für Entwicklung (DSE).

12 The contemporary history of PETA is excellently described in Maria Luisa Torres Reyes, 1997: 61–8.

13 Not to be confused with the Indian People's Theatre Association (IPTA) (1941–56) as founded during the 1940s in India, nor with the Indigenous People's Theater Association (IPTA).

14 For an impression of the meeting in Bangladesh, see: K. Epskamp, 1983. For a report on the Namibia meeting, see: K. Epskamp, 1993. This article is also available in Epskamp 1992: 229–37.

15 The source of some of the information on IDEA is the IDEA website.

16 PETA was inspired by the American Creative Dramatics approach and published a modest Trainers' manual, *Creative Dramatics* (Hong Kong: Plough Publications, 1981). Much has been written about PETA in the Philippines, while Eugène van Erven has documented and advocated the PETA experiences for an international readership. PETA's 'people-based aesthetics' – Creative Dramatics – grows from the participants. According to Kao and O'Neill (1998: 2–3), Winnifred Ward of Northwestern University established Creative Dramatics as an important part of the education of pupils and of their teachers during the 1920s and 1930s. Originating from children's play, its justification comes from the principles of child-centred Progressive Education. There were similar developments in Britain during the 1940s and 1950s, when spontaneity, creativity, self-expression and personal growth were the goals of drama in education, rather than formal presentations and the acquisition of theatre skills and knowledge.

17 Atelier-Théâtre Burkinabè (ATB) in Burkina Faso produces plays dealing with children's

154

conditions and issues (such as health, children working in gold mines, the problem of street children, and unemployment).

18 The play 'I Will Marry When I Want' was banned by the government in November 1977. Its author, Ngugi (born in 1938 in Limuru, Kenya), was arrested and spent the whole of 1978 in prison.

19 MERCOSUR consists of Argentina, Chile, Paraguay, Uruguay and Brazil. Peru, Bolivia, Ecuador, Colombia and Venezuela are organised in the Andes Pact.

20 An anthropological definition of development might refer to the improvement of the quality of life, while an economist's definition easily takes refuge in the numbers and figures of quantitative research.

21 The community as a social formation possesses a cultural depth, typified by history lived on known ground, and by a common memory and a sense of belonging, of identity. This may be manifested, for example, in a feeling of identity or in common behaviour, as well as in activities and territory. When the community refers to a shared territory, such as a neigh-bourhood, a hamlet, a village, a block, or a suburb, a community may be defined geographically as a local group or social unit, occupying a local space within a defined physical area. A community may also refer to the people related to an institution like a church, a school or a hospital. Within the context of development cooperation, community is often defined in terms of target group(s) or 'primary stakeholders', such as refugees, tribal people, coloured people, youth, street children, juvenile delinquents, women or landless labourers.

22 Economists speak of 'human capital' to indicate that knowledge is a stock of value generating a flow of value. In general, economic capital is a stock that will generate a flow of economic values (Klamer, 2002).

23 This distinction between A, B and C cultures, as launched in 1997 by Everitt (for the Council of Europe) was made earlier by Professor P. Thoenes in *Van Wetenschap tot Utopie; Opstellen voor Overmorgen* (1976), though Everitt makes no reference to Thoenes's work.

24 Cultural identity is a fluid, volatile concept. The Council of Europe (1997: 45) takes it to signify the use of coded, expressive modes of behaviour or communication, including language, dress, traditional kinship patterns, institutions, religion and the arts.

25 In the the 1970s and 1980s the discipline of development studies drew a distinction between two different approaches to development. The first approach stemmed from the autonomous processes of change which, at the community level, originated inside-out and was referred to as 'endogenous' development. The second approach was project-oriented and based on outside intervention. Initiatives here originated from decisions which were 'foreign' to the community or target group. In such a context, this is known as 'exogenous' development.

26 The Dutch Department of Development Cooperation co-financed two international seminars organised by the International Popular Theatre Alliance (IPTA) in Dhaka (Bangladesh) in 1982 and in Rehoboth (Namibia) in 1991. As we have seen, both initiatives received technical assistance from the International Council for Adult Education in Toronto.

27 The English version of this report was published in 1991. See pp. 190–3 for the section on 'Culture and Development'.

28 On p. 11 of the SIDA report reference is made to strengthening the status of cultural develop-ment cooperation by supporting programmes that: (1) strengthen the cultural infrastructure; (2) promote artistic training, competence development, and sharing of experience; (3) build up regional and international networks; (4) contribute towards the upgrading of the status of culture and the cultural worker among politicians, those in power, and decision makers; (5) result in legislation within cultural areas – for example, copyrighting, illegal export of cultural objects, and preservation of culturally valuable sites; and (6) lead to the establish-ment of a cultural policy in countries where no such policy exists.

29 'In seeking to raise the awareness of Council staff about opportunities for "arts for develop-ment" activity, this study does not mean to devalue or undermine traditional arts work. There are advantages in achieving a balance between "arts for development" and the arts purely as an information tool.' (Butchard, 1995: 2)

30 HIVOS (2002: 3) adheres to a definition of culture as a broad and dynamic concept referring to people's practices, values, beliefs and aspirations, and to how they shape their existence.

31 'Activities that make use of the arts in a purely instrumental way to raise awareness about particular problems, like for instance educational theatre about AIDS/ HIV, or educational documentaries about human rights violations, gender inequality or other social issues, do not qualify for support under the arts and culture programme. When particular projects not

falling under the arts and culture policy criteria are deemed valuable from the perspective of awareness raising, HIVOS can consider supporting these programmes via one of the other HIVOS sectors.' (HIVOS, 2002: 11)

32   In line with this September 1998 event, the Inter-American Development Bank organised an 8–12 March 1999 meeting in Paris in close collaboration with UNESCO that also focused on culture and development. And in October that same year UNESCO joined forces with the World Bank and the Italian Government to organise an international conference in Florence, to demonstrate that 'Culture Counts'.

33   'In discussing cultural policy, it is useful to make a clear distinction between arts policy that concerns the promotion of the arts in general and artists policy which pertains to a direct improvement of artists' economic and social conditions, which usually includes taxation, social security, and labour conditions.' (Watanabe, 1996: 155)

34   Historical archives are perceived as 'monuments to the passage of time', in contributing not only to institutional memory but also in capturing the social memory of society at large.

35   Chapter 11 discusses various forms and characteristics of art education, with examples from several developing countries.

36   The Jomtien Declaration (1990) can be seen as the culmination of contemporary international educational thinking based on 1980s practices. Education for All – or Basic Education, as it is commonly known – is very closely related to basic learning needs, covering the knowledge and skills which children as well as adults need to lead a decent life. The concept of basic education was to embrace a series of learning tools and modalities. Basic education refers to any education, formal or non-formal, intended to develop the knowledge, skills, attitudes and values necessary for people to survive, to function in the local community, to improve the quality of their lives and to continue learning. In this way basic education includes various, sometimes sequential, forms of education.

37   The Fifth World Conference on Adult Education (CONFINTEA V), Hamburg (1997).

38   The information on 'participatory training' presented here is mainly taken from Binoy Acharya and Shalini Vermal, 1994: 8.

39   By means of ice-breaking games participants are introduced to the basic elements of drama: role, character, situation, human interaction, voice, movement, language, dramatic tension, text, etcetera.

40   This formulation of action research has been taken from information provided by Centre for the Arts in Development Communications (CDC, Winchester) on TfD.

41   Through improvised and scripted drama the participants learn to communicate meaning through expression and interpretation.

42   Source: brochures and personal correspondence with the Darpana Academy of Performing Arts.

43   Oral literature is also referred to as 'orature', literature as an oral experience. In Africa, as all over the world, literature has to be performed to become familiar in the ears of an audience.

44   The stigmatisation and discrimination associated with HIV/AIDS prevent a great many of the 40 million people with HIV/AIDS around the world from seeking treatment for and information about the disease. The shame associated with the pandemic is such that many are even afraid to take an AIDS test.

45   The first steps in initiating this Theatre Unit at the NFED towards launching the TfD programme is described in detail by Osita Okagbu, 'Product or process: Theatre for Development in Africa', *African Theatre for Development; art for Self-determination*, edited by Kamil Salhi (Exeter: Intellect 1998), pp. 32–4.

46   See 'Roots of community theatre' (van Erven, 2001: 1–3).

47   After the starting of the dialogue on peace negotiations in Oslo, and between the agreements signed in Washington on 13 September 1993 and in Cairo on 13 September 1994.

48   Strengths, Weaknesses, Opportunities and Threats (SWOT).

49   Logical framework analysis is a systematic tool for project planning based on an internally coherent set of questions and answers. It is a planning tool to be employed after the stake-holder analysis has been conducted. (Seppälä and Vainio-Mattila, 2000: 40). More information on the logical framework can be found in Chapter 7, which discusses conventional development planning and management processes.

50   As Prentki (1998: 421) writes: 'Facilitators need time to integrate themselves into the community to the level where the most marginalised gain the trust and confidence to

undertake an active role in the process.'

51 This definition is taken from Srilatha Batliwala, quoted in Medel-Anonuevo (1997: 83).

52 cdcArts is located within the School of Community and Performing Arts at King Alfred's College.

53 For information on the MA programme see: www.kingalfreds.ac.uk/postgraduate/ index.htm and www.cdcArts.org

54 'Though, of course, not new to individual artists, research, in both its natural and social science senses, is a relative novelty at art schools.' See Schneider (1996: 197).

55 Ferruccio Marotti, related to the Centro Teatro Ateneo, is the leading professor in the field of Balinese theatre.

56 Professor Eckhard Breitinger is the coordinator of African Theatre Studies at Bayreuth University.

57 The information on the National Centre for Performing Arts (Bombay, now Mumbai) is taken from written communication with the Assistant Director of Programmes and Personal Relations, S.Y. Rege, dated 31 January 1995.

58 Several case studies are presented in Chapter 6 of Mlama's *Culture and Development; the Popular Theatre Approach in Africa* (1991) such as 'Theatre for Social Development' (TSD; 1982-1983), the Bagamoyo popular theatre workshop (1983), the Msoga popular theatre workshop (1985) and the Mkambalani popular theatre workshop (1986).

59 Deutsche Gesellschaft für Technische Zusammenarbeit (GTZ). The planning and management method of GTZ is known as 'Zielorientierte Projekt Planung' (ZOPP).

60 *Ex ante* and *ex post* evaluations are also referred to as formative and summative types of evaluation.

61 'Best practices' are documented strategies and tactics employed by successful projects or programmes.

62 In tracer studies, the effects of the training or education on the performance, the attitude or the career of the trainee are measured some time after the training has been completed.

63 A comprehensive discussion of development support communication media and their applications can be found in Boeren, 1994.

64 The model comes in many forms and variations, ranging from quite simple (involving no intermediate steps in the communication process between sender and receiver) to very complicated and sophisticated variations (involving and showing as many intermediate steps as possible).

65 These ways of communicating have been the subject of study of 'semiotics', the inter-disciplinary study of culturally determined systems of signs.

66 Everett M. Rogers used a diffusionist model of development communication. See: Singhal and Rogers (1989; 1999). Programmes reviewed include *Soul City, Hum Log, Dialogo, Twende na Wakati* and *Simplemente Maria.*

67 'Entertainment-education' has also been referred to as 'edutainment' or 'infotainment'.

68 Examples are available from Lorna Cromwell: cromwell@population.org

69 In South Africa soaps are referred to as *sepies*. At the beginning of the 1990s the first indigenous soap series was produced, called *Egoli*. It turned out to be extremely popular, not only in South Africa but in the whole of Africa south of the Sahara.

70 Writers invited were (among others) Delia Fiallo, Miguel Sabido, Fernanda Villeli, Sergio Vainman, Gloria Perez, Mariela Romero, Benedicto Roy Barbosa and Martha Bossia.

71 Persuasion (by means of campaigns, for example) leads to short-term behavioural changes – and needs to be repeated to gain sustainability.

72 Rights such as copyright and intellectual property rights, and values such as the rejection of plagiarism and forgery.

73 Source: Brochures and written communication with the Darpana Academy of Performing Arts.

74 This information originates from an interview held with M. Berman (1984: 26–7).

75 Akademi Seni Karawitan Indonesia.

76 Akademi Seni Tar Indonesia.

77 Institut Kesenian Jakarta.

78 The English ballet dancer Catherine Geach was the initiator of this school. Since then it has been visited by many well-known people including the Dutch pianist Cor Bakker, and is funded through the Dutch NGO Mensen in Nood.

79 The self-governing region of Nunavut was established in 1999.

80 These tapes may be ordered through Loukie Levert, Van Boetzelaerlaan 184, 2581 BA The Hague, The Netherlands.
81 In November 2002 the e-book was published on the Internet.
82 Within the field of education and training final evaluations are made by means of formal tests and examinations. The results of education and training projects in particular require long-term evaluation, for example by conducting surveys on former students' careers. Tracer studies are an effective instrument to track down career developments.
83 The Manchester University Drama Department was founded in 1961 as the result of a generous gift from Granada Television.
84 Well known students who graduated or obtained a PhD from the School of English (Leeds University) include Jacob Srampickal. His modified version of his PhD was published as paperback *Voice to the Voiceless; the Power of People's Theatre in India* (Srampickal, 1994).
85 This MA course takes advantage of its close working relationship with scholars and practitioners of international repute from all the great world traditions of dance, theatre and performance. In addition to such practitioners as Phillip Zarrilli and Richard Schechner actually teaching and working on the course for extensive periods of time, the CPR invited guest-lecturers like Rustom Bharucha, Guillermo Gomez-Pena, Peggy Phelan, Barbara Kirshenblatt-Gimblett, Peter Sellars, Mike Pearson, Jatinder Verma, Kristin Linklater and Enrique Pardo.
86 Established in 1981.

Bibliography

Acharya, Binoy and Shalini Vermal (1994), 'Participatory training for social development', *Rural Extension Bulletin*, 6 (December): 8–12.

Akolo, J. B. (1987), 'Art education and cultural imperatives', *Nigeria Magazine*, 55, 2: 20–9.

Andreasen, John (1996), 'Community plays – a search for identity', *Theatre Research International*, 21, 1: 72–8.

Avenstrup, R. (1991), 'Opening the schools to arts and culture: a challenge to curriculum reform', in *Culture in Namibia: an Overview*, Windhoek: Swedish International Development Authority (SIDA), pp. 56–60.

Banya, K. and J. Elu (1997), 'Implementing basic education: an African experience', in *International Review of Education*, 43, 5/6: 481–96.

Barley, Nigel (1983), *The Innocent Anthropologist: Notes from a Mud Hut*, London: British Museum.

Bastos Barbosa, A.M.T. (1992), 'The role of education in the cultural and artistic development of the individual: developing artistic and creative skills', paper presented at the UNESCO International Conference on Education (43rd session), International Conference Centre (Geneva), 14–19 September 1992.

Beattie, Donna Kay (1996), 'Objects of assessment: what aspects of learning effects do we assess: products and/or processes', in *Art and Fact: Learning Effects of Arts Education*, Utrecht: Netherlands Institute for Arts Education. (Proceedings of an International Conference, Rotterdam, 27–28 March 1995.)

Belisle, Rachel, Dipta Bhog and Ingrid Jung (1997), 'Participation and partnership, sustainability and transferability', in Werner Mauch and Uta Papen (eds.) *Making a Difference: Innovations in Adult Education*, SCO Institute for Education/the German Foundation for International Development, pp. 181–90.

Berman, M. (1984), 'Cultuur- en kunstonderwijs slaat brug tussen traditioneel en modern; Papua New Guinea en de kunst van het overleven', in *Overzicht*, 14, 2: 48–9.

Beukes, Leon (1991), 'Grassroots theatre in Namibia', in *Some Essays on the Cultural Life in Namibia*, Windhoek: Ministry of Education and Culture, pp. 21–2.

—— (1991), 'Community and grassroots theatre in Namibia', in *Culture in Namibia: an Overview*, Windhoek: Swedish International Development Authority (SIDA), pp. 69–70.

Blaustein, S. (1989), 'The Khmer renaissance: Hun Sen's government seeks legitimacy as the preserver of the nation's culture', in *Far Eastern Economic Review* (Hong Kong), 145, 38: 44–6.

Boal, Augusto (1979), *Theatre of the Oppressed*, New York: Urizen Books.

—— (1995), *The Rainbow of Desire*, London: Routledge.

Boeren, Ad (1994), *In Other Words ... the Cultural Dimension of Communication for Development*, The Hague: Centre for the Study of Education in Developing Countries (CESO).

—— (1995), 'The code for development: communication and culture', in Manfred Oepen (ed.), *Media Support and Development Communication in a World of Change: New Answers to Old Questions?* Berlin: Appropriate Communication in Development (ACT)/Freie Universitat Berlin/Worldview International Foundation, pp. 180–5. (Proceedings of an International Conference, Berlin, 19–20 November 1993.)

—— (2000), 'The sectoral cakewalk: finding a balance between programme ownership and the need for technical assistance', in Kees Epskamp (ed.) *Education in the South: Modalities of International Support Revisited.* The Hague: Nuffic, pp. 29–45.

Bollag, Burton (2002), 'Dramatic intervention', in *Chronicle of Higher Education*, 21 June.

Borofsky, R. (1998), 'Cultural possibilities', in *Culture, Creativity and Markets: World Culture Report 1998,*. Paris: UNESCO, pp. 64–75.

Bramwell, Roberta and Kathleen Foreman (1993), 'Questioning power structures and competitiveness in pedagogy; insights from North American Indian and Philippine pedagogies', in *Inter-*

159

national Review of Education, 39, 6: 561–75.

Breitinger, Eckhard (ed.) (1994), *Theatre and Performance in Africa: Intercultural Perspectives* (Bayreuth African Studies, No. 31), Bayreuth: Bayreuth University/Institute for African Studies.

Burkey, Stan (1993), *People First: a Guide to Self-reliant Participatory Rural Development*, London/New York: Zed Books.

Butchard, Tim (1995), *The Arts and Development; a Study of the Interface between Culture and Development, and of the Implications for the British Council's Arts Work in Developing Countries*, British Council.

Byam, Lee Dale (1999), *Community in Motion: Theatre for Development in Africa*, Critical Studies in Education and Culture series, edited by Henry A. Giroux, Westport and London: Bergin & Garvey.

Canadian International Development Agency (CIDA) (1991), *Society, Culture and Sustainable Development; a Discussion Paper*, International Economic Analysis Unit (Policy Branch), 27 July.

—— (1995), *Involving Culture: a Fieldworkers' Guide to Culturally Sensitive Development*. Contribution to the UNESCO research programme on the integration of cultural factors in development plans and projects. Paris, UNESCO.

Chambers, Richard (1994a), 'The origins and practice of participatory rural appraisal', in *World Development*, 22, 7: 953–69.

—— (1994b), 'Participatory rural appraisal (PRA): analysis of experience', in *World Development*, 22, 9: 1253–68.

—— (1994c), 'Participatory rural appraisal (PRA): challenges, potentials and paradigm', in *World development*, 22, 10: 1–17.

Consuegra, M., K. Mazrui and J. Müller (n.d.), 'The needs issue', in Werner Mauch and Uta Papen (eds.), *Making a Difference: Innovations in Adult Education*, Frankfurt am Main: Peter Lang Europäischer Verlag der Wissenschaften, pp. 191–6.

Copeland, Roger (1983), 'Post-modern dance, post-modern architecture, post-modernism', in *Performing Arts Journal*, 7, 1: 27–43.

Corhay, J. M. (1993), 'Indigenous peoples', *The Courier*, 140: 72–3.

Cornwall, A. and R. Jewkes (1995), 'What is participatory research?', in *Soc. Sc. Med.*, 41, 12: 1667–76.

Council of Europe (1997), *In From the Margins: a Contribution to the Debate on Culture and Development in Europe*, Strasbourg, the European Task Force on Culture and Development.

Country report of Indonesia (1990), in *Final Report of the SPAFA Consultative Meeting on Research on Textbooks Development for Art Education in Southeast Asia* (S-R281), 11–15 February 1990, Bangkok, Suansunandha Teachers' College Auditorium. (Appendix 6; SPAFA/301.8/WS23/90; ISBN 974-7809-30-3).

Crego, Ch. and G. Groot (1985), 'Pierre Bourdieu en de filosofische esthetica; aantekeningen bij het nawoord van La Distinction', in *Algemeen Nederlands Tijdschrift voor Wijsbegeerte* (Assen), 77, 1: 21–35.

Dagrón, Gumucio A. (2001), *Making Waves: Stories of Participatory Communication for Social Change*, New York: Rockefeller Foundation Report.

de Hegedus, P. (1995), 'The concept of evaluation and how it relates to research', in *Adult Education and Development*, 44: 61–73.

Delannoy, M. (1995), 'Shakespeare's Romeo en Julia in tweetalige Israelisch-Palestijnse co-produktie', in *Mabat: Cultuur, Wetenschap en Kunst in Israel*, 28: 4–6.

Demirbas, N. and M. Rabbae (1990), 'Intercultureel onderwijs en kunstzinnige educatie', in *Kunsten & Educatie, Tijdschrift voor Theorievorming*, 3, 3: 8–16.

DGIS/Ministry of Foreign Affairs (1991), *A World of Difference; a New Framework for Development Cooperation in the 1990s*, The Hague: Staatsuitgeverij/Ministry of Foreign Affairs.

—— (1995), *De Herijking van het Buitenlands Beleid*. The Hague: Ministry of Foreign Affairs.

Donelan, Kate (1999), 'The drama of ethnography', in Carole Miller and Juliana Saxton (eds.), *Drama and Theatre in Education: International Conversations*, Victoria BC: International Drama in Education Research Institute (IDERI), pp. 256–64.

Dors, H. G. (1990), 'Kunstzinnige educatie in multi-etnisch perspectief', in *Kunsten & Educatie, Tijdschrift voor Theorievorming*, 3, 3: 24–32.

Dubbelboer, Janneke and Vivian Paulissen (1995), 'Representation and value education via television in Mexico', in Leo Dubbeldam (ed.), *Values and Value Education*, The Hague: Centre for the Study of Education in Developing Countries (CESO), pp. 75–91.

Dubbeldam, Leo and Kees Epskamp (eds.) (1996), *Searching Together: an Anthropology of Educational Research in China and the Netherlands*, The Hague: Centre for the Study of Education in Developing Countries (CESO).

Eade, Deborah (1997), *Capacity-building: an Approach to People-centred Development*, Oxford: Oxfam.

El-Amari, Lamice (1998), 'East meets West in Arab theatre', in Ria Lavrijsen (ed.), *Global Encounters in the World of Art: Collisions of Tradition and Modernity*, Amsterdam: Royal Tropical Institute (KIT), pp. 51–64.

Elu, Juliet and Kingsley Banya (1999), 'Non-governmental organizations as partners in Africa: a cultural analysis of North–South relations', in Kenneth King and Lene Buchert (eds.), *Changing International Aid to Education: Global Patterns and National Contexts*, Paris: UNESCO, pp. 182–206.

Epskamp, Kees (1983), 'Getting popular theatre internationally organised', in *Sonolux Information*, no. 11, December.

—— (1989), *Theatre in Search of Social Change: the Relative Significance of Different Theatrical Approaches*, The Hague: Centre for the Study of Education in Developing Countries (CESO), (CESO Paperback no. 7).

—— (1992), *Learning by Performing Arts: from Indigenous to Endogenous Development*, The Hague: Centre for the Study of Education in Developing Countries (CESO), (CESO Paperback no. 16).

—— (1993), 'Playing in a sandpit: international popular theatre meeting in Namibia', *South African Theatre Journal*, 7, 1: 7–15.

—— (1994), 'The role of education in cultural and artistic development', in *International Yearbook of Education*, 44: 158–72.

—— (1999), 'Healing divided societies', in *People Building Peace: 35 Inspiring Stories from Around the World*, Utrecht: European Centre for Conflict Prevention in cooperation with IFOR.

—— (2000), 'Capacity building within the context of the Sector Wide Approach (SWAp) to development', in Kees Epskamp (ed.), *Education in the South: Modalities of International Support Revisited.*, The Hague: Netherlands Organisation for International Cooperation in Higher Education (Nuffic) (Nuffic paperback no. 3).

—— (2000), 'Community theatre: local and national identity building', in John O'Toole and Margret Lepp (eds.) *Drama for Life: Stories of Adult Learning and Empowerment*, Brisbane: Playlab Press, pp. 125–34.

Etherton, Michael (1969), 'A popular theatre for Zambia: the Kasama theatre workshop', in *Bulletin International Social Research*, pp. 13–21.

—— (1972), 'Zambia: popular theatre', in *New Theatre Magazine*, 12, 2: 19–21.

—— (1980), 'Popular theatre in Kaduna State, Nigeria, the work of the Ahmadu Bello University Drama Collective 1977–1980'. Paper delivered to the International seminar on The Use of Indigenous Social Structures and Traditional Media in Non-formal Education and Development, organised by DSE and ICAE, 5–12 November, Berlin (West).

—— and Brian Crow (1979), 'Wasan Manoma; community theatre in the Soba District of Kaduna State', *Savanna* (Ahmadu Bello University, Zaria), 8.

Everitt, Anthony (1999), *The Governance of Culture: Approaches to Integrated Cultural Planning and Policies*, Strasbourg: Council of Europe/Cultural Policies Research and Development Unit (Policy Note, no. 5).

Feral, J. (1997), 'Pluralisme in de kunst of interculturalisme?', in F. Mayor (ed.), *De Kracht van Cultuur*, The Hague: Directie Voorlichting Ontwikkelingssamenwerking/ Ministerie van Buitenlandse Zaken, pp. 118–25.

Figueroa, Maria Elena, D. Lawrence Kincaid, Manju Rani and Gary Lewis (2002), *Communication for Social Change: an Integrated Model for Measuring the Process and Its Outcomes*, New York: The Rockefeller Foundation, Communication for Social Change Working Paper Series, no. 1.

Fordham, P., D. Holland and J. Millican (1995), *Adult Literacy: a Handbook for Development Workers*. Oxford and London: Oxfam and Voluntary Service Overseas.

Freire, Paolo (1968), *Pedagogy of the Oppressed*, New York: Seabury Press.

Galla, Amareswar (1995), 'Arts, culture, human rights and democracy', in *Bringing Cinderella to the Ball: Papers Presented at a Conference on Arts and Culture in the New South Africa*, Johannesburg: Cosaw Publishing/National Arts Coalition (NAC).

Ganzeboom, Harry B. G. (1996), 'Effects of arts education in primary and secondary education on cultural consumption and socio-economic careers in later life', in *Art & Fact: Learning Effects of Arts Education*, Utrecht: Netherlands Institute for Arts Education (LOKV), pp. 146–56. (A collection of lectures given during the two-day international conference Art & Fact, 27–28

March 1995, World Trade Center Rotterdam).

Gecau, K., V. Chivaura and S. Chifunyisé (1991), *Community Based Theatre in Zimbabwe: an Evaluation of Zimfeps's Experiences*, Harare: Zimbabwe Foundation for Education and Production.

Geertz, Clifford (1996), *After the Fact: Two Countries, Four Decades, one Anthropologist*, Cambridge, MA: Harvard University Press.

Goblot, E. (1973), 'Cultural education as a middle-class enclave', in E. Burns and T. Burns (eds.), *Sociology of Literature and Drama*, Harmondsworth, UK: Penguin Books, pp. 433–44.

Gould, Helen (2001), 'Culture and social capital', in Francois Matarasso (ed.), *Recognising Culture: a Series of Briefing Papers on Culture and Development*, London: Comedia, Department of Canadian Heritage/UNESCO, pp. 69–75.

Hall, Edward T. (1969), *The Hidden Dimension*, New York: Anchor Books.

Harding, Francis (1999), 'Fifteen years between: Benue and Katsina workshops, Nigeria', in Martin Banham, James Gibbs and Ferni Osofisan (eds.), *African Theatre in Development*, Oxford and Bloomington: James Currey and Indiana University Press.

HIVOS (2002), *Policy Document Arts and Culture: Towards Cultural Diversity and Pluralism*, The Hague: HIVOS.

Inayatullah (1967), 'Toward a non-western model of development', in Daniel Lerner and Wilbur Schramm (eds.), *Communication and Change*, Honolulu: East-West Center, pp. 98–102.

Iriarte, Patricia (1993), 'El poder sutil de la telenovela', in *Chasqui*, 47: 91–2.

Isar, Yudhishthir Raj (2000), 'Cultural policies for development: tilting against windmills?', in *Culturelink*, special issue 2000, 15–20.

Jackson, Anthony R. (1997), 'Positioning the audience: interactive strategies and the aesthetic in educational theatre', *Theatre Research International*, 22: 1, 48–60.

Jackson, Tony (ed.) (1993) *Learning Through Theatre: New Perspectives on Theatre and Education*, London and New York: Routledge.

Jentzsch, Konrad (1996), 'Arts education programmes in Germany', in *Art and Fact: Learning Effects of Arts Education*, Utrecht: Netherlands Institute for Arts Education (LOKV), pp. 184–97. (A collection of lectures given during the two day international conference Art & Fact, 27–28 March 1995, World Trade Center Rotterdam.)

Kamlongera, Christopher (1989), *Theatre for Development in Africa, with Case Studies from Malawi and Zambia*, Bonn: Education Science and Documentation Centre.

Kann, Ula (1999), 'Aid co-ordination in theory and practice: a case-study of Botswana and Namibia', in Kenneth King and Lene Buchert (eds.), *Changing International Aid to Education: Global Patterns and National Contexts*, Paris: UNESCO, pp. 239–54.

Kao, Shin-Mei and Cecily O'Neill (1998), *Words into Worlds: Learning a Second Language Through Process Drama*, London: Ablex Publishing Corporation.

Keregero, K. J. B. and M. M. Keregero (1991), 'Participatory action research: enabling scientists to empower the rural poor', in B. Hoeper (ed.), *Qualitative Versus Quantitative Approaches in Applied Empirical Research in Rural Development*, a documentation of the workshop at Sokoine University of Agriculture, Morogoro, Tanzania, 21–26 May 1990, Bonn: Deutsche Stiftung für internationale Entwicklung (DSE), pp. 84–104.

Kerr, David (1999), 'Art as tool, weapon or shield? Arts for Development Seminar, Harare', in Martin Banham, James Gibbs and Femi Osofisan (eds.), *African Theatre in Development*, Oxford and Bloomington: James Currey and Indiana University Press, pp. 79–86.

—— and Chifunyise, Stephen (1984), 'Popular theatre in Zambia: Chikwakwa reassessed', *Théâtre International*, 11/12, 3/4: 54–80.

Kidd, Ross (1979), 'Liberation or domestication: popular theatre and non-formal education in Africa', *Educational broadcasting international*, 12, 1: 3–9.

—— (1980), 'People's theatre, adult education and social change in the third world'. paper prepared for the international seminar on the Use of Indigenous Social Structures and Traditional Media in Non-Formal Education and Development, organised by ICAE and DSE, Berlin, November.

—— (1982), *The Popular Performing Arts, Non-formal Education and Social Change in the Third World: a Bibliography and Review Essay*, The Hague, CESO (CESO Bibliography no. 7).

—— (1982), 'Botswana, Nigeria: participatory drama, popular analysis and conscientising the development worker', in *Reading Rural Development Communication Bulletin* (RRDC), no. 16, December: 19–25.

—— (1982), 'Liberation or domestication: popular theatre and non-formal education in Africa', in *Young Cinema and Theatre*, 4: 8–17.

—— (1982), 'Popular theatre and popular struggle in Kenya: the story of Kamiriithu community educational and cultural centre', in *Theaterwork* 2, 6: 47–61.

—— (1984), *From People's Theatre for Revolution to Popular Theatre for Reconstruction: Diary of a Zimbabwean Workshop*, The Hague, CESO. (CESO Verhandelingen no. 33)

—— (1992), 'Popular theatre for reconstruction in Zimbabwe', in Ad Boeren and Kees Epskamp (eds.), *The Empowerment of Culture: Development, Communication and Popular Media*. The Hague: The Centre for Education in Developing Countries (CESO), pp. 127–45.

—— and Martin Byram (1977), 'Popular theatre and development: a Botswana case study, *Convergence* 10: 2, 20–30.

—— and Martin Byram (1978), 'Popular theatre as a tool for community education in Botswana', in *Assignment Children: a Journal Concerned with Children, Women and Youth in Development* (UNICEF), 44: 35–66.

—— and Martin Byram (1978), *Popular Theatre: a Technique for Participatory Research*. Toronto, Participatory Research Project (Working Paper no. 5).

—— and Nat Colletta (1980), *Tradition for Development: Indigenous Structures and Folk Media in Non-formal Education*. Berlin and Toronto: German Foundation for International Co-operation (DSE) and the International Council for Adult Education (ICAE)paper prepared for the international seminar on the Use of Indigenous Social Structures and Traditional Media in Non-Formal Education and Development, organised by ICAE and DSE, Berlin, November.

Klaic, Dragan (1998), 'Unlike airlines and phone companies; performing arts in Europe', in Peter B. Boorsma, Annemoon van Hemel and Niki van der Wielen (eds), *Privatization and Culture; Experiences in the Arts, Heritage and Cultural Industries in Europe*. Boston/Dordrecht/London: Kluwer Academic Publishers, pp. 170–82.

—— (1999), 'Close encounters; European internationalism', *Theater*, Yale University, School of Drama, 29, 1: 115–28.

Klamer, Arjo (ed.) (1996), *The Value of Culture: on the Relationship between Economics and Arts*, Amsterdam: Amsterdam University Press.

Klamer, Arjo (2002), 'Accounting for social and cultural values', in *The Economist*, 150, 4: 453–73.

Kleymeyer, Charles David (1993), 'Cultural expression and grassroots development', in Charles David Kleymeyer (ed.). *Cultural Expression and Grassroots Development; Cases from Latin America and the Caribbean*. Boulder/London: Lynne Rienner, pp. 195–214.

Kloos, Peter (1995), 'Cultuur in ontwikkeling', in G. Thijs (ed.), *Cultuur, Identiteit en Ontwikkeling*, (Themabundel ontwikkelingsproblematiek, no. 6), Amsterdam: VU uitgeverij, pp. 24–41.

Kress, G. (1996), 'Internationalisation and globalisation: rethinking a curriculum of communication', *Comparative Education*, 32, 2: 185–96.

Lavrijsen, Ria (1998), 'Introduction', in Ria Lavrijsen (ed.), *Global Encounters in the World of Art: Collisions of Tradition and Modernity*. Amsterdam, Royal Tropical Institute, pp. 9–28.

Leach, Edmund (1973), 'Ourselves and the others', *Times Literary Supplement*, 6 July, 771.

Leis, Raul A. (1979), 'The popular theatre and development in Latin America', *Educational Broadcasting International*, 12, 1: 10–13.

—— (1980), 'La palabra nueva del pueblo', *Media Development*, 27, 3: 15–19.

Warren Linds (1999), 'The metaxic journey of the drama facilitator/inquirer', in Carole Miller and Juliana Saxton (eds.), *Drama and Theatre in Education: International Conversations*. Victoria BC: International Drama in Education Research Institute (IDERI), pp. 271–9.

Loopuyt, M. (1990), 'De muziekschool in Fez; Marokko', in *Wereldmuziek* (Amsterdam), 1, 5: 6–7.

Makagiansar, M. (1981), 'Some notions on "exotic countercurrents of culture"', in F. Derks (ed.), *De Exotische Tegenstroom*, The Hague: National UNESCO Commission, The Netherlands, pp. 13–27.

Makon, K. (1991), 'Prague puppeteers expand training focus', in *EuroMaske, the European Theatre Quarterly*, Winter 1990/91, no. 2.

Marranca, B. (1991), 'Thinking about interculturalism', in B. Marranca and G. Dasgupta (eds.), *Interculturalism and Performance*. New York: Performing Arts Journal, pp. 9–23.

Matarasso, François (2001), 'Culture, economics and development', in François Matarasso (ed.) *Recognising Culture: a Series of Briefing Papers on Culture and Development*, London: Comedia/Canadian Heritage/UNESCO, pp. 3–10.

—— and Charles Landry (1999), *Balancing act: 21 Strategic Dilemmas in Cultural Policy*. Strasbourg, Council of Europe/Cultural Policies Research and Development Unit (Policy Note, no. 4).

Mattern, M. (1997), 'Popular music and redemocratization in Santiago, Chile 1973– 1989'. *Studies in Latin American Popular Culture*, 16: 101-113.

Mavrocordatos, Alex (1995), 'Rise Namibia: uncover the covered'. Report on the CLT Training Programme, Karas and Hardap regions, February 1993–May 1995. n.p.

Maybury-Lewis, David (1997), *Indigenous People, Ethnic Groups, and the State*. Boston/London: Allyn and Bacon.

McKinley, T. (1998), 'Measuring the contribution of culture to human well-being: cultural indicators of development', in *Culture, Creativity and Markets; World Culture Report 1998*, Paris: UNESCO, pp. 322–31.

McQuail, D. (1997), *Audience Analysis*. London: Sage Publications.

Mda, Zakes (1993) *When People Play People; Development Communication Through Theatre*, London and Johannesburg: Zed Books and Witwatersrand University Press.

Medel-Anonuevo, Carolyn (1997), 'Learning gender justice: the challenge for adult education in the 21st century', *Background Papers CONFINTEA V, July 1997*. Bonn and Hamburg: Institute for International Co-operation of the German Adult Education Association (IZZ/DVV) and UNESCO Institute for Education (UIE). (Special issue of *Adult Education and Development*, no. 49, 1997, pp. 5–299.)

Mensah, John Victor (1997), 'Getting the people to participate; community animation in Ghana', in *D+C*, no. 4, 20–1.

Mlama, Penina Muhando (1991), *Culture and Development; the Popular Theatre Approach in Africa*. Uppsala: Scandinavian Institute of African Studies.

Mundy, Simon (2000), *Cultural Policy; a Short Guide*. Strasbourg, Council of Europe/Council for Cultural Co-operation/Cultural Policy and Action Department Research and Development Unit.

Musa, Bala A. (1998), 'Popular theatre and development communication in West Africa: paradigms, processes and prospects', in Kamal Salhi, *African Theatre for Development: Art for Self-determination*, Exeter: Intellect, pp. 136–54.

Namulondo Nganda, C. (1996), *Primary Education and Social Integration; a Study of Ethnic Stereotypes in the Ugandan Basic Test Books for Primary School English and Social Studies*, Bayreuth, Bayreuth University. (Bayreuth African Studies, no. 38).

Nelson, Nici and Wright, Susan (1995), 'Participation and power', in Nici Nelson and Susan Wright (eds.), *Power and Participatory Development: Theory and Practice*, London: Intermediate Technology Publications, pp. 1–18.

Ngugi wa Thiong'o and Ngugi wa Mirii (1982), *I Will Marry When I Want*, African Writers Series, no. 246, London: Heinemann.

Niehof, Anke (n.d.), 'De culturele dimensie van ontwikkeling', in *De lange adem: slagen en falen in de praktijk van de ontwikkelingssamenwerking*. The Hague: Voorlichtingsdienst Ontwikkelings-samenwerking, Ministry of Foreign Affairs, pp. 91–7.

Nitulescu, Virgil Stefan (2002), 'Cultural policies: Romania, an insight view', in *ABLAK, Magazine for Central-Europe and the Balkans*, 7, 2: 6–8.

Okagbu, Osita (1998), 'Product or process: Theatre for Development in Africa', in Kamil Salhi (ed.), *African Theatre for Development: Art for Self-determination*, Exeter, UK: Intellect, pp. 23–41.

Ong, Walter J. (1993), *Orality and Literacy: the Technologizing of the Word*, London: Routledge.

O'Toole, John and Margret Lepp (eds.) (2000), *Drama for Life: Stories of Adult Learning AND Empowerment*, Brisbane: Playlab Press.

Peacock, James L. (1986), *The Anthropological Lens: Harsh Light, Soft Focus*, New York: Cambridge University Press.

Plastow, Jane (1998), 'Uses and abuses of Theatre for Development: political struggle and development theatre in the Ethiopia-Eritrea war', in Kamal Salhi (ed.), *African Theatre for Development: Art for Self-determination*, Exeter, UK: Intellect, pp. 97–113.

Prentki, Tim (1998), 'Must the show go on? The case for Theatre for Development', *Development in Practice*, 8, 4: 419–29.

Rahnema, M. (1990), 'Participatory action research: the "last temptation of saint" development', *Alternatives, Social Transformation and Human Governance*, 15, 2: 199–226.

Rao, J. Mohan (1998), 'Culture and economic development', in M. Couratier and M.Quinn (eds.), *Culture, Creativity and Markets; World Culture Report 1998*, Paris: UNESCO.

Rea, K. (1979), 'Theatre in India: the old and the new, part IV', *Theatre Quarterly*, 9, 34: 53–65.

Reform and Transition; the Future of Repertory Theatre in Central and Eastern Europe, n.d., n.p. (Report of a workshop held in Prague, 21–24 November 1996).

Rockefeller Foundation (1999), *Communication for Social Change: a Position Paper and Conference*

Report. New York: Rockefeller Foundation.

—— (1999), *Communications and Social Change: Forging Strategies for the 21st Century*, New York: Rockefeller Foundation.

Rogers, Alan (1992), 'Training for literacy: the problem with Freire', *Adult Education and Development*, 39 (1992): 132–42.

Rogers, Everett M. (1995), *Diffusion of Innovations*, fourth edn. New York: Free press.

—— and F. Shoemaker (1971), *Communication of Innovation: a Cross-cultural Approach*. New York and London: The Free Press and Collier McMilan Publishers (first edition, 1962).

Rosenblum, P. (1981), 'The popular culture and art education', in *Art Education: the Journal of the National Art Education Association*, 34, 34.

Roussel, Gilles (1995), 'Enterprising Africa; culture: a key factor in development', *The Courier*, 152 (July–August): 100–1.

Saavedra, Rosa and Miryan Zuniga, Maria Linnea, (Ging) Tanchuling, Uta Papen (1997), 'Conversation on empowerment', in Werner Mauch and Uta Papen (eds), *Making a Difference: Innovations in Adult Education.*, Peter Lang/UNESCO, pp. 197– 215.

Salhi, Kamal (ed.) (1998), *African Theatre for Development*. Exeter, Intellect Books.

Schechner, Richard (2002), *Performance Studies; an Introduction*. London/New York: Routledge.

Schneider, Arnd (1996), 'Contemporary artists and anthropology: uneasy relationships', *Journal of Material Culture*, 1, 2: 183–210.

Seppälä, Pekka and Arja Vainio-Mattila (2000), *Navigating Culture; a Road Map to Culture and Development*, Helsinki: Ministry for Foreign Affairs, Department for International Development Cooperation.

Serageldin, Ismail (1991), 'Banking on culture; the director of the World Bank's Africa Department discusses the issue', in *UNESCO Sources*, 25 (April), p. 10.

Serageldin, Ismail (1998), 'Culture and development at the World Bank', published in *Urban age* (special issue on 'Cultural heritage').

Serageldin, Ismail and J. Taboriff (1992), *Culture and development in Africa*, Washington DC: World Bank.

Sharp, Caroline (1990), 'Artists in schools: issues and implications', in *Educational Research*, 32, 2: 140–3.

SIDA (1995), *The Role of Culture in Development*, Stockholm: Department for Democracy and Social Development/Division for Culture and Media/Education Division, SIDA.

Singhal, Arvind and Everett M. Rogers (1989), 'Educating through television', *Populi*, 16, 2: 38–47.

—— (1999), *Entertainment-Education: A Communication Strategy for Social Change*. Lawrence Erlbaum Associates.

Slim, Hugo and Paul Thompson (1993), *Listening for a Change: Oral Testimony and Development*, London: Panos Publications.

Snir, Reuven (1996), 'Palestinian theatre as a junction of cultures. The case of Samih al-Qasim's Qaraqash', in *Journal of Theatre and Drama* (JTD), University of Haifa, 2 (1996): 101–20.

SPAFA (1990), Country report of Indonesia in *Final Report of the SPAFA Consultative Meeting on Research on Textbook Development for Art Education in SouthEast Asia* (S-R281). 11–15 February, Bangkok.

Squarci, L. (1993), 'What are minorities; some possible criteria', *The Courier*, 140 (July–August): 50–2.

Srampickal, Jacob (1994), *Voice to the Voiceless; the Power of People's Theatre in India*, New Delhi: Manohar Publishers.

Srampickal SJ, Jacob and Richard Boon (1998), 'Popular theatre for the building of social awareness: the Indian experience', in Richard Boon and Jane Plastow (eds), *Theatre Matters: Performance and Culture on the World Stage*, Cambridge: Cambridge University Press, p. 135–53.

Theons, P. (1976), *Van Wetenschap tot Utopie. Opstellen voor OvermorgeN*, Meppel/Amsterdam: Boom.

Thompson, L. (1989), 'A foot in the past, a foot in the future', *Pacific Islands Monthly* (Suva, Fiji), 59: 48–9.

Tohmé, G. (1992), *Cultural Development and Environment*. Paris and Geneva: UNESCO and International Bureau of Education (IBE).

Torres Reyes, Maria Luisa (1997), 'Theatre as an encounter of cultures', in *Theatre Research International*, 22: 1, 61–8.

Ugwu, Catherine (1998), 'The art of conflict', in Ria Lavrijsen (ed.), *Global Encounters in the World of Art: Collisions of Tradition and Modernity.* Amsterdam: Royal Tropical Institute, pp. 67–77.

UNESCO/World Commission on Culture and Development (1995), *Our Creative Diversity.* Report of the World Commission on Culture and Development. France: EGOPRIM.

UNESCO (1998), *Culture, Creativity and Markets; World culture report 1998.* Paris. (UNESCO World Culture Report no. 1).

UNESCO (1998), *Intergovernmental Conference on Cultural Policies for Development; final report.* Paris, UNESCO.

UNESCO/Inter-American Development Bank (1999), 'The value of culture; position paper from the Forum "Development and Culture"', presented at the meeting 'The value of culture', organised by the Inter-American Development Bank and UNESCO, Paris, 11–12 March 1999.

UNESCO (2000), *Cultural Diversity, Conflict and Pluralism: World Culture Report 2000.* Paris (UNESCO World Culture Report no. 2).

UNESCO/UNESCO Sector for Culture (2001), 'Culture throughout the project cycle', in François Matarasso (ed.), *Recognising Culture: a Series of Briefing Papers on Culture and Development.* London: Comedia/Canadian Heritage/UNESCO, p. 77–88.

Van Erven, Eugène (1987a), 'Philippine people's theatre down under', *New Theatre Australia,* 2 (December): 33–7.

—— (1987b), 'The theatre of liberation of India, Indonesia and the Philippines', in *Australasian Drama Studies,* 10 (April): 3–19.

—— (1987), 'Philippine political theatre and the fall of Ferdinand Marcos', in *The Drama Review,* 114 (Summer): 56–70.

—— (1987), 'Theatre of liberation in action: PETA and the people's theatre network of the Philippines', in *New Theatre Quarterly,* 3, 10: 131–49.

—— (1989), *Stages of People Power: the Philippines Educational Theatre Association.* The Hague, CESO. (CESO Verhandelingen no. 43)

Van Erven, Eugène (1992), *The Playful Revolution: Theatre and Liberation in Asia.* Bloomington, Indiana University Press. 304 pp.

—— (2001), *Community Theatre: Global Perspectives,* London/New York: Routledge.

Van der Jagt, Marijn (1987a), 'Ideeën Augusto Boal: poging toeschouwers te bereiken via andere theatervormen; problemen, uitspraken oplossingen', *Speltribune,* September: 3–5.

—— (1987b) 'Augusto Boal achterhaald; de fictie van het forum-theater', in *Toneel Teatraal* 108, 4: 31–2.

Van Herk, Hannie and Marijke De Vos (1985), 'Zweeds theatermaakster in Afrika; Martha Vestin, Friteatern', in *Toneel teatraal,* 106: 6, 36–8.

Van Veghel, J. (1990), 'Het herstel van de Kambodjaanse cultuur', in *Internationale Samenwerking,* 10: 10–11.

Watanabe, M. (1996), 'In search of a cogent cultural policy; observations on the findings of US/Japan Cultural Policy Study, 1993–1995'. *Culturelink,* 18: 143–70.

Weitz, S. (1988), 'Performing arts education and the school system in Israel', in *Canadian and International Education,* 17, 2: 48–60.

Wolcott, H. F. (1995), *The Art of fieldwork.* Walnut Creek/London: Altamira Press (a division of Sage publications).

Wright, H. K. (1994), 'Educational change in Sierra Leone: making a case for critical African drama', in *International Journal of Educational Development,* 14, 2: 177–94.

Yeomans, R. (1994), 'Islamic art in the primary classroom', in *Muslim Education Quarterly,* 11, 2: 52–6.

Index

Abah, Steve 15
Acharya, Binoy 156
ACPC (Action for Cultural and Political
  Change) (India) 55
action research 2, 47-50, 52, 79, 156
activist's theatre 9
Adehyeman 56
adult education 60, 69-70, 81, 86, 89, 115,
  117, 120, 123, 131, 154
adult educators 3, 9, 20, 58, 69
Africa viii-ix, 2, 4, 14-17, 19, 21, 23, 39,
  56, 58, 74, 81-4, 92, 110, 119, 137
African Centre for the Training of Performing
  Arts (ACTPA) 137
African Research and Educational Puppetry
  Programme (AREPP) 139
African Theatre Exchange ATEX() 137
Ahmadu Bello University 14, 84
Al-Kasaba Theatre company 61
animators 5, 10, 17-18, 69, 76, 77
anthropology x, 1, 3, 29, 35, 48, 89, 128,
  155
Aranyak theatre group 17
architecture 30, 39, 148
Argentina 1, 111, 155
art education xi, 156, 6, 39, 41, 52, 83, 84,
  118-29
Artpad 20, 78
Asia xvi, 1, 15, 17, 23, 41, 54, 56, 59, 79,
  125, 129, 151
Atelier-Théâtre Burkinabè (ATB) 20, 155
attitudes 2, 31, 45, 57, 61, 65, 66, 68-70,
  74, 75, 81, 89, 91, 102, 109, 111, 122,
  124, 130, 156
audio-visual media 20, 40, 107

Avenstrup, R. 128
awareness raising 3, 5, 6, 9, 10, 12, 13, 17,
  27

Bagamoyo theatre workshop 157
BaMa 41
Bangladesh 15, 16, 17, 57, 155
Baniel, Eran 61
Banya, K. 114
baseline survey 6, 102
basic education 24, 41, 52, 60, 81, 124-6,
  128, 131, 134, 156
basket funding 98
Bastos Barbosa, A.M.T. 120, 126
Batliwala, Srilatha 157
belief systems 54, 128
beliefs 4, 29, 31, 61, 65, 150
Belisle, Rachel 26
benchmark surveys 6, 102
Beukes, Leon 59
Bhog, Dipta 126
Boal, Augusto 1, 9, 12-14, 20
Boeren, Ad ii, 158
Brazil 1, 9, 10, 20, 78, 111, 155, 159
Brecht, Bertolt 12-14, 60
British Council (BC) 35
British American Arts Association (BAAA)
  151, 153
Buenaventura, Enrique 154
Burkey, Stan 70, 154
Butchard, Tim 35, 156
Byam, Lee Dale 19, 20, 154

Cabrujas, José Ignacio 111
Cambodia 132-3, 134

167

theatre and development xiv, 11, 44, 76, 78, 149
Theatre-in-Education (TIE) 11, 14
Third World xiv, xv, 1, 78, 158
Thoenes, P. 155
Thompson, L. 125
Tohmé, G. 126
Topiaco, Soxy 139
tourism 38, 129

UNESCO 16, 32, 34, 36-7, 88, 101, 105, 129, 137, 151-2, 156, 160
University of Dar es Salaam 82
University of Namibia 82, 83
University of Toronto 15
University of Zambia 14

Vainio-Mattila 22, 64, 70
Vainman, Sergio 111, 158
values 28-31, 34, 45, 54, 61, 71, 74, 109, 111, 118, 120, 156, 158
Van der Jagt, Marijn 14
Vermal, Shalini 156
visual arts 34-5, 39, 42, 60, 82-3, 132, 134, 152

Watanabe, M. 38, 124, 156
WCCD (World Commission on Culture and Development) 32, 34
WDCD (World Decade for Cultural Development) 88
Weitz, S. 125
West Indies 58
Windhoek 82, 133
workshops xi, 3, 9, 14-20, 44, 46, 47, 49-50, 52, 56, 58, 63-5, 66-70, 72
World Bank 15, 24, 36-7, 88, 98, 156
Wright, Susan 70, 74
Wright, H. K. 119

Z
Zambia 14, 15, 17, 138
Zambian National Theatre Arts Assocation (ZANTAA) 17
Zimbabwe 15-17, 20, 137
Zimbabwean Association of Community Theatre (ZACT) 17, 152
ZOPP 157